CATULLUS

ANCIENTS IN ACTION

CATULLUS

Amanda Kolson Hurley

BRISTOL CLASSICAL PRESS

First published in 2004 by
Bristol Classical Press
an imprint of
Gerald Duckworth & Co. Ltd.
90-93 Cowcross Street, London EC1M 6BF
Tel: 020 7490 7300
Fax: 020 7490 0080
inquiries@duckworth-publishers.co.uk
www.ducknet.co.uk

A catalogue record for this book is available
from the British Library

ISBN 1 85399 669 6

Acknowledgements

The author is grateful to Charles Martindale for his insightful comments on a draft of the manuscript.

An earlier version of part of the Conclusion appeared in *Omnibus*, September 2001.

All translations, unless otherwise stated, are the author's.

With two exceptions – widely anthologized pieces by Edmund Spenser and John Addington Symonds – quotations of English poetry are taken from Julia Haig Gaisser's splendid collection *Catullus in English* (Penguin, 2001).

The author is grateful to Faber & Faber Ltd and Grove Atlantic for permission to quote from Tom Stoppard, *The Invention of Love*, © Tom Stoppard 1997.

Typeset by e-type, Liverpool
Printed and bound in Great Britain by
CPI Bath

Contents

To Lawrence
because you've always regarded my trifles as *something*.

Introduction

In Tom Stoppard's recent play *The Invention of Love*, the protagonist, 77-year-old poet and classical scholar A.E. Housman (referred to in the play as 'AEH'), lies in a hospital bed dreaming that he has died and gone to Hades, the underworld of ancient mythology. In Hades he meets a young version of himself (referred to in the play as 'Housman'). This young man, not recognising his interlocutor, tells 'AEH' of his aspiration to become both a great poet and a great scholar, and asks:

Housman: Can't one be both?

AEH: No. Not of the first rank. Poetical feelings are a peril to scholarship. There are always poetical people ready to protest that a corrupt line is exquisite. Exquisite to whom? The Romans were foreigners writing for foreigners two millenniums ago; and for people whose gods we find quaint, whose savagery we abominate, whose private habits we don't like to talk about, but whose idea of what is exquisite is, we flatter ourselves, mysteriously identical with ours.

Housman: But it is, isn't it? We catch our breath at the places where the breath was always caught. The poet writes to his mistress how she's killed his love – 'fallen like a flower at the field's edge where the plough touched it and passed on by'. He answers a friend's letter – 'so you won't think your letter got forgotten like a lover's apple forgotten in a good girl's lap till she jumps up for her mother and spills it to the floor blushing crimson over her sorry face'. Two thousand years in the tick of a clock – oh, forgive me, I …

AEH: No (need), we're never too old to learn.

Housman: I could weep when I think how nearly lost it was, that apple, and that flower, lying among the rubbish under a wine-vat, the last, corrupt, copy of Catullus left alive in the wreck of ancient literature. It's a cry that cannot be ignored.[1]

The poet of whom 'Housman' speaks is Catullus, and this interchange between 'Housman' and 'AEH' vividly captures the dispute that has polarised interpretation of Catullus for the past two centuries. The young Housman, on the one hand, reads the poetry of Catullus as if it were the heartfelt cry of a living person. Invoking two similes used by Catullus himself, he describes the text in organic terms, as 'that apple, and that flower'; though 'corrupt' (that is, rife with copyists' errors), it is nevertheless very much alive. The antiquity of the poems does nothing to dampen 'Housman''s strong feelings of empathy for their author. Like so many readers since, he marvels that a single, tattered copy of Catullus' book survived the Middle Ages (supposedly at the bottom of a wine-vat). And he thrills at the transparency, the immediacy of Catullus' verse: 'Two thousand years in the tick of a clock' simply vanish, he feels, making Catullus his own contemporary. For 'Housman', then, Catullus' poetry is evidence of the timelessness of the human emotions.

'AEH', on the other hand, scoffs at the idea of an essential or unchanging human nature. He points out that if people never really changed through the ages, their aesthetic criteria would not change, either. Yet we know that our tastes are not identical to those of the Greeks or of the Romans. 'There are always poetical people ready to protest that a corrupt line is exquisite. Exquisite to whom?' he demands. We would be obtuse, he implies, to suppose that the Romans, 'whose gods we find quaint, whose savagery we abominate', could have shared our idea of beauty. But the old Housman is not as cynical as he professes to be. Clearly he is moved by 'Housman''s impassioned appeal, conceding, 'we're never too old to learn'.

Many readers of Catullus today, I think, would sympathise with 'Housman'. Of course we see the truth in the observation made by 'AEH' that 'The Romans were foreigners writing for foreigners two millenniums ago'. Nevertheless it is still largely his directness, or the *impression* of his directness, that makes Catullus popular with a modern audience. Like most poets of this century and the last, Catullus habitually writes in the first-person voice about his own experiences: coming home to his beloved lakeside villa (poem 31); chastising a friend for betraying him (poem 30 and poem 77); being spurned by a girlfriend (poem 8) or boyfriend (poem 99). He dissects his emotions, and often expresses them in hyperbolic terms; because they are extreme they seem all the more 'real'. Tellingly, almost all of the poems by Catullus that are most popular today – those numbered 5, 7, 11, 31, 85, 101 and a handful of others – concern love and/or friendship, and most are narrated in the first person. Catullus' emotional honesty – whether real or imagined – attracts us to him. In *The Invention of Love*, it moves 'Housman' to tears, and even touches a nerve in the cantankerous 'AEH'.

Sincerity has long been considered the chief hallmark, and virtue, of Catullus' poetry. In their 1908 school edition of Catullus, for example, H.V. Macnaghten and A.B. Ramsay declared that 'there is no author ... who is more convincingly simple and sincere ... who never disguises his feelings, and always speaks from the heart'.[2] Yet this sincerity is more problematic than it appears at first glance. When Catullus 'confesses', he does so in an oblique or disjointed way; we are left with the impression of a partial and fragmented autobiography, while there is little solid evidence on which to base it.

Take, for example, what is now the best-known of Catullus' poems, that numbered 85:

I hate and I love. Why do I do this, you may ask?
I don't know, but I feel it happen, and it tortures me.

This poem has long been celebrated for its pithiness, which is inarguable, and its autobiographical candour, which I would like to call into question. For what does Catullus actually reveal here? His conflicting emotions, certainly, and his helplessness in the face of them. But whom, or what, does he simultaneously love and hate? And why does he harbour these warring passions – what occasion has prompted the poem? We aren't told, or offered any clues. And besides, who is the 'you' Catullus addresses – any reader, in the present or future? Or someone specific, who knows the intimate details of the poet's situation? All of this is unclear. The reader's sense of confusion is heightened by the poet's admission of his own ignorance: 'I don't know', he writes, why he feels this way.

One time-honoured strategy for reading Catullus has been to rearrange the poems in such a way that they seem to tell the poet's life-story, and to take the resulting 'autobiography' as dramatic context. On this model, the catalyst behind the emotions voiced in poem 85 can be found in another poem – in, for example, poem 58, in which Catullus claims that his girl-friend Lesbia cheats on him with other men at crossroads and in alleyways; or in poem 72, which draws a distinction between the affection Catullus once felt for Lesbia and the burning but contemptuous lust he feels for her at the time of writing. Once the context of poem 85 has been established, we might try to determine the next incident in the 'plot', the event that poem 85 itself gives rise to: a good candidate might be poem 11, where

Catullus asks his friends to bid his mistress a cold farewell on his behalf. Of course, this mode of reading has its drawbacks. For one thing, there is no internal evidence in poem 85 that the object of Catullus' love and hate is Lesbia – or anyone else in particular.

If we lifted poem 85 out of the 'storyline', what would we be able to say about it? Surprisingly, quite a lot. We might compare it to other poems in which Catullus employs juxtaposition: poem 47, for instance, which contrasts the unscrupulous henchmen Socration and Porcius (nicknamed by the poet 'Itch' and 'Hunger') with Catullus' friends Veranius and Fabullus. We might consider its style: the simple, colloquial language that is so tightly structured, the intimate tone, and the poet's use of the forceful verb *excrucior* ('I am crucified').

In that it invites interpretation from many angles, poem 85 is a typical Catullus poem – if any of his poems can be called 'typical', for the Catullan corpus is astonishingly diverse. Its 116 poems can be sorted into three basic groups: 'polymetrics' (poems numbered 1-60), or poems in a wide variety of metres; long poems (61-8); and 'elegiacs' (69-116), mostly short epigrams all composed in elegiac couplets. Not that they fall very easily into these categories, which are by no means discrete or self-contained. There are countless stylistic and thematic affinities between poems in different parts of the corpus, more than enough to complicate the organising principle of metre. The 'Lesbia cycle', which spans all three categories, still seems to many readers the most obvious and coherent grouping in the whole body of work.

Apart from those twenty-six poems about Lesbia, Catullus wrote an *epyllion* or mini-epic on the mythical wedding of Peleus and Thetis (64); a long poem in the rare galliambic metre about Attis, a devotee of the fierce goddess Cybele (63); two epithalamia, or wedding songs (61 and 62); two long poems on the death of his brother (65 and 68A); a Hellenistic-style poem on the mythical lock of Berenice, a queen of Ptolemaic Egypt (66); a dialogue between a lover and the door of his mistress' house (67); and eighty-two more polymetrics and epigrams, which one scholar, Amy Richlin, classifies into these additional sub-groups: 'Out of all the polymetrics and epigrams', she notes, 'sixty-two – well over half – include invective or sexual material, some of the coarsest in Latin verse …. Of approximately forty invective poems, ten excoriate thieves of one sort or another, while several others threaten sexual rivals of the poet or people who have been unfaithful to their lovers.'[3] Catullus' poetry, then, is an extra-ordinary farrago of different styles, themes and genres.

The diversity of the poems is reflected by Catullus' unusual reception in the English-speaking world. In the five hundred years since his poetry arrived in Britain, no major English-language writer has translated the whole of the *liber Catulli* (book of Catullus), or even a substantial portion of it. Instead writers have isolated small groups of poems, or sometimes just odd verses, for translation or imitation. In this book I quote liberally from the best Catullan writings in English, in order both to supplement my own functional translations of the Latin, and to demonstrate how ardently and sensitively some of the greatest English writers have responded to Catullus' poems.

In recent years, diverse interpretive approaches under the umbrella of Critical Theory have greatly enhanced our under-standing of Catullus' work and world. Gender studies has offered us new perspectives on those of his poems that deal with sexual desire, and on the (sometimes bewildering) variety of gender roles he assumes. Psychoanalytic theory has shed light on our own habits of reading Catullus, especially the tendency for readers to rearrange the poems into an 'autobiography' of the author. Ancient history and archaeology continually provide us with new evidence for Roman society and culture in the first century BC. My aim here is not to evaluate these approaches or to advance one above the rest, but to try them out in a more experimental spirit, making use of them as they seem relevant to a given text. However, my primary critical tool in these pages is close reading of Catullus' poetry, which all readers can apply with success.

Catullus the poet is a tangle of contradictions: erudite, obscene, arch, passionate, boastfully aggressive, abjectly self-pitying. As for Catullus the man, his life is the subject of Chapter 1.

1

Between Myth and History:
The Life of Catullus

Historical evidence

With their provocative silences and half-confessions, Catullus'
poems are sometimes a maddening tease. We can't help but
wonder what Catullus was really like. Nor can there be any question that many of the themes in his poetry were derived from his
personal life. Fortunately, historical evidence for Catullus' life
does survive (other ancient poets, like the satirist Juvenal, were
not so lucky). But the evidence should not be regarded as a
neutral record – for even this history has been unalterably tinged
by the myth that has grown up around Catullus.

St Jerome (mid-fourth century to early fifth century AD)
states in his *Chronicle* that Gaius Valerius Catullus[1] was born in
Verona in 87 BC and died at Rome in his thirtieth year (i.e. in
58-57 BC). However, Catullus' poem 11 includes a reference to
Julius Caesar's expeditions to Britain, which took place in 55-54
BC, while poem 113 alludes to the second consulship (the
highest political office in Rome, with a one-year term) of the
general Pompey in 55; either Catullus was born after 87 BC, or
Jerome is wrong about his age at death (or both). Most scholars
give Jerome the benefit of the doubt and round Catullus' dates
up to 84-54 BC. The belief that Catullus died young has been a
significant factor in the reception of his poetry since the nineteenth century. It provides a fittingly tragic ending to the story

of tortured love-sickness presented in the Lesbia poems. It also lends an extra poignancy to Catullus' grief at the untimely death of his brother – for the reader 'knows' that Catullus was to share the same fate. Yet at least one prominent scholar, T.P. Wiseman, finds the evidence for Catullus' early death unconvincing, and argues that the poet may have lived on to write mimes.[2]

In his *Lives of the Caesars* (*Deified Julius* 73), the biographer Suetonius (born *c.* AD 70) writes:

> Valerius Catullus, as Caesar did not deny, set a lasting brand on Caesar with his verses about Mamurra; but when Catullus made amends, he invited him to dinner the same day, and, as he had become accustomed to the hospitality of Catullus' father, so he continued to enjoy it.

Suetonius alludes to the several insulting poems that Catullus directs at Mamurra, Julius Caesar's chief engineer in Gaul, whose immense (and, according to Catullus, ill-gotten) wealth was legendary. One of these poems (57) also attacks Caesar; we can only guess how he initially responded to it. The most significant detail in Suetonius' account is the friendly relationship he says existed between Caesar and Catullus' father. This means that Catullus' family was almost certainly aristocratic, though not top-tier *nobiles*.

In poem 31, Catullus calls himself the 'master' of his home Sirmio. Sirmio (modern Sirmione) is a peninsula on Lake Garda near Verona in the north of Italy. It seems reasonable to assume that Catullus' family would have owned all, or most, of the peninsula: three miles long and narrow, it could not have supported much more than one sizeable estate.

Verona and its environs were subjugated by the Romans only in 101 BC; its settlements (in some cases, mere outposts) became

Latin colonies in 89 BC, a few years before Catullus was born. Before it came under Roman control, northern Italy – known then as Cisalpine Gaul – was home to an assortment of Celtic tribes that were culturally and ethnically distinct from the Romans. When in 101 BC the Roman army defeated a force of invading Cimbri, a people from northern Gaul, veterans from the winning side received parcels of land in the conquered territory. T.P. Wiseman suggests that Catullus' grandfather may have been one of the ex-soldiers, or one of the many central Italian entrepreneurs who also ventured into this frontier country at the beginning of the first century BC.

What does Catullus' background in Cisalpine Gaul tell us about him? Not that he was a country bumpkin: on the contrary, his command of Greek was assured, which indicates that he was well-educated. In the ancient Roman world, education for the elite normally consisted of Greek and Latin poetry, rhetoric and philosophy. The *Transpadani* (those who lived on the northern side of the River Po; Catullus labels himself a *Transpadanus* in poem 39) seem to have had strong trading links with Greece and the East, and were, like the central Italians, considerably Hellenised.

Nevertheless, we should remember that Verona was ten days' journey from Rome by cart. In spite of his aristocratic, Roman-citizen family and his Greek learning, Catullus may have looked a bit foreign to Roman eyes. Indeed, to many Romans, Cisalpine Gaul (or the Italian countryside in general) was an old-fashioned place, where the traditional morals of honest farmers held sway. Roman writers of the late Republic and early Empire often favourably contrasted provincial virtues – industry and piety – with the idleness, avarice and luxury that ran rampant in the *urbs* (city). Of course, they were in large part indulging their nostalgia for the old Italy of yore (the way modern city-dwellers might romanticise Highland crofters as holdovers from 'simpler times'). But their accounts did, to some extent, reflect social reality. Rural society was agriculture-based, and the country gentry actively engaged in farming and trade – unlike in Rome, where the leading families shunned commerce.

At some point Catullus went to live in Rome. We can surmise that he made his primary residence there on the basis of poem 68A, a 'letter' from Verona, in which Catullus explains to his friend Manlius that he hasn't composed any poems recently because his books are all at home in Rome. (That Catullus should apologise for not writing verse *in a poem* is an irony typical of him.) Once in Rome, Catullus formed friendships with notable men, including fellow poets. He addressed poems to Asinius Pollio (poem 12), an historian and consul in 40 BC; to C. Licinius Calvus (poems 14, 50, 53 and 96), a famous orator and poet; and even to the great orator Marcus Tullius Cicero (poem 49), who was about twenty years Catullus' senior. Cornelius Nepos – author of the mammoth biographical work *On Illustrious Men*, now mostly lost, and the entirely lost *Chronicle* – is the dedicatee of the volume of poems.

Along with Calvus, Nepos and others, Catullus belonged to a group or school of modernising poets, referred to by Cicero as the *poetae novi* (new authors) and *neoteroi*. The 'neoterics' looked for inspiration to the Hellenistic poets who flourished from the third to the first century BC, primarily Callimachus of Cyrene, Apollonius of Rhodes, Theocritus and Meleager. (The studied elegance of their Greek style is often termed 'Alexandrian', after the centre of Hellenistic literary activity.) Among the Alexandrian ideals that Catullus and his peers adopted was verbal innovation – coining new words and using slang or dialect-words in place of more 'literary' alternatives (so Catullus famously imported a slang word for 'kiss', *basium*, into Latin literature). The neoterics also drew from Hellenistic poetry a general preference for short genres over long ones, for wit and polish over heavy solemnity. In poem 95, for example, which praises the mini-epic *Zmyrna* (now lost) by his friend Helvius Cinna, Catullus proclaims (9-10), 'My comrade's small monument is close to my heart; / Let the crowds delight in bloated Antimachus'. (The poet Antimachus was criticised by Callimachus in similar terms.)

Was this a 'revolution in Roman poetry', as Kenneth Quinn asserted in his influential 1959 book *The Catullan Revolution*?[3] It is difficult to assess the legacy of Catullus' fellow neoterics because so little of their work survives. But these writers undoubtedly made a great contribution to Roman literature by broadening its spectrum, from its early traditions of epic (pre-eminently Ennius' *Annales*, from the early second century BC) and drama, to include new kinds of lyric and iambic poems as well as narrative elegy, epigram and the epyllion. To say that the neoterics paved the way for the Augustan poets of the next two generations – Horace, Virgil, Ovid, Propertius, Tibullus – is obviously correct, but it risks misrepresenting their achievements as a rough beginning, a mere 'first draft' of Augustan literature. In fact they were artful writers who set a new stylistic standard in Latin and demonstrated the possibilities of working in 'slight' genres.

So the neoterics formed part of Catullus' social milieu. Then, of course, there was 'Lesbia' – if she was indeed a real person.[4] Our crucial source for the identity of the historical 'Lesbia' is the second-century AD North African writer Apuleius, author of a picaresque novel, the *Metamorphoses* (also called *The Golden Ass*), and a courtroom oration known as the *Apologia*, in which he defends himself against a charge of using magic to seduce a wealthy widow. (The trial took place in AD 158; because the speech was eventually published we can assume that his defence was successful.) In one of the *Apologia*'s many digressions, Apuleius remarks (10):

> You've also noticed that I'm blamed because, although these boys go by other names, I call them 'Charinus' and 'Critian'. On this same principle people may make accusations against the works of others: Gaius Catullus, because he used the name 'Lesbia' for Clodia ... and Propertius, who, saying 'Cynthia', protects Hostia; and Tibullus, because Plania is in his heart, but 'Delia' in his verse.

Taking their cue from this passage, Latin scholars – beginning with Antoine Muret in 1554 – have identified Lesbia as Clodia Metelli, the strong-willed noblewoman denounced by Cicero in his speech *Pro Caelio* (*In Defence of Caelius*). Clodia Metelli was a member of the blue-blooded Claudian family and the wife of high-ranking government official Metellus Celer. According to Cicero, Clodia had had an affair with the young orator M. Caelius Rufus, and then accused him of trying to poison her. The poison-plot was almost certainly a fabrication, and there is no mention of it in Catullus' poems; some scholars find evidence for the Caelius-Clodia affair, however, in Catullus' apostrophe at poem 58, line 1 – 'Caelius, our Lesbia, *that* Lesbia' – which may suggest that Catullus and his friend Caelius were both romantically involved with Lesbia. Whether this Caelius is Caelius Rufus is not clear (though in poem 77 Catullus complains that a certain Rufus has betrayed him).

The attractive theory that Lesbia = Clodia Metelli gains support from poem 79, which begins with the statement 'Lesbius is pretty', or in Latin, *Lesbius est pulcher*. Clodia Metelli had a famous brother, the demagogue P. Clodius Pulcher. If he were 'Lesbius' to his sister's 'Lesbia', then Catullus' epithet 'pretty' (*pulcher*) would be a revealing pun on Clodius' name. But, as Wiseman points out, Clodia Metelli had two sisters, both of whom used the unconventional spelling 'Clodia' instead of 'Claudia'. Was Apuleius actually referring to one of these two women?

Lesbia's historical identity will probably never be firmly established. Nevertheless, Lesbia/Clodia has in modern times developed into a vibrant, fully-rounded literary character, appearing in numerous works of historical fiction. (Of these the most notable is Thornton Wilder's novel *The Ides of March*, in which her fickleness is put down to childhood sexual abuse at the hands of an uncle.)

Another intriguing 'absent presence' in Catullus' verse is the poet's brother, who died before him and left him badly bereaved. Poem 101 is Catullus' famous elegy for this brother, ostensibly delivered at the brother's gravesite overseas (more precisely, at Troy, according to poems 65 and 68B). Catullus describes the pain of his 'long grieving' in poem 65, characterising his brother as *amabilior vita*, 'more beloved than life'. Clearly this relationship was a significant one for Catullus, but regrettably we know nothing about the poet's brother, not even his full name.

'Let's fly off to the famed cities of Asia', Catullus writes in poem 46. Several of the poems indicate that Catullus travelled to Asia Minor on the staff of a Roman government official. In poem 10 the poet mentions Bithynia (a province in northern Asia Minor, in modern-day Turkey), implying that he has recently returned from there; in poem 28 he complains about having served under a greedy praetor (magistrate) named Memmius. We know, on the authority of a letter from Cicero to his brother Quintus, that Memmius was praetor at Rome in

58 BC; if Memmius had taken up a provincial governorship after his one-year praetorship, as was the custom, then he (and, presumably, Catullus) would have been in Bithynia in 57-56 BC. Appointments such as Catullus' were common among young upper-class men in Rome, eager to see the far corners of Rome's dominions and make some money from 'perks' associated with the collecting of tribute. (In some cases, this meant ruthless extortion, though evidently Catullus did not profit from his time in Bithynia.) Not long after returning from Asia, if we believe Jerome, Catullus died. In support of Jerome's account is the fact that none of Catullus' poems alludes to events that took place after 54 BC.

The picture I have just sketched of Catullus may look depressingly incomplete. In fact, we know more about Catullus' life than we do about the lives of most ancient authors (Sappho, for example, is an obscure figure, while the identity of Homer – probably a composite – is a total mystery). And we are lucky to know what we do, for Catullus survived into the modern age by the most tenuous of threads. By the early fourteenth century, all traces of him had vanished – except for a single manuscript, the one allegedly discovered at the bottom of a wine-vat. This manuscript disappeared again quickly, but not before copies were made. However, the text was a hopeless mess: by one modern editor's estimate it contained 1,000 errors. We owe our more or less accurate text to the fifteenth- and sixteenth-century European humanists who purged the corpus of scribal mistakes. Their contribution cannot be underestimated: before their careful editing, many of the poems were run together, which resulted in jarring shifts in address, tone and argument.

Some verses were rendered utterly nonsensical by even the tiniest of scribal slips. For example, one problematic verse from poem 61 stood as *sed michi ante labello* ('but for me before

[your] lip[s]'?) until 1577, when the redoubtable humanist Joseph Scaliger intuited that the first three words (*sed michi ante*) were in fact a corruption of one compound word in Latin, *semihiante*, 'half-open'. In a brilliant stroke Scaliger emended the line to *semihiante labello*, 'with half-open lips', a graceful phrase that is perfectly appropriate to its context – a description of a smiling baby. In his poem 'The Scholars' (1915), W.B. Yeats represented such editorial labours, undertaken by 'Old, learned, respectable bald heads' (2), as anathema to Catullus' spirit (1-6; 11-12):

> Lord, what would they say
> Did their Catullus walk that way?

Yet it is the combined efforts of the 'bald heads' and of imaginative non-scholars like Yeats that make reading Catullus so rewarding today.

Catulluses

Every generation of readers during the last two centuries has tried to get at the life 'behind' Catullus' art – at the motives or situations that gave rise to sentiments such as those voiced in 85. So, on the basis of their favourite Catullus poems, readers will often conjure up a personality for the poet, a subjective idea of who Catullus was. The whole corpus can then be interpreted according to how well it reflects one's own 'Catullus'.

Although they proliferate all the time, these imagined Catulluses are not wildly idiosyncratic. A community of readers who share the same aesthetic values will also tend to latch on to the same aspects of Catullus' poetry. So, for example,

Renaissance poets were drawn to the wedding poems 61 and 62, while eighteenth-century English readers took a special interest in Catullus' epigrams. Broadly speaking, the Catulluses of the last 150 or 200 years conform to the following three types:

1. Romantic Catullus. This Catullus owes something to popular perceptions of Shelley and Byron: he is politically radical, emotionally unstable, and follows his instincts (literary and sexual) as opposed to society's conventions. Romantic Catullus has a sensitive temperament, and is quick to flare up in feelings of love, hate or despair (the last especially at his brother's death). Hence, he usefully 'explains' one unusual aspect of the Catullan corpus – its vacillation between tenderness and obscene abuse. Lesbia, on the Romantic view, simply could not appreciate the sublimity of Romantic Catullus' love; nor could his friends, who had baser dispositions.

According to this theory, Catullus' long poems are of secondary importance, or are even dismissed as contrived and pretentious. Because Catullus' temperament was mercurial – so the theory goes – his special gift was for composing short lyrics, for quickly capturing his emotions before they gave way to new ones. The critic E.A. Havelock, in his influential 1939 book on Catullus, went so far as to maintain that 'his genius [is] lyrical, in the sense that he could not write anything significant which was not essentially a quick mood expressed within narrow limits'.[5] Such neglect of the long poems is an unfortunate, but common, by-product of the 'Romantic Catullus' paradigm. Another is misogyny: because Catullus is assumed to be sincere, it follows that the historical Lesbia must actually have been as fickle and promiscuous as he claims. A third problem with this model is its privileging of one of Catullus' literary exemplars – Sappho, the seventh-century BC lyric poet

– over others who are equally, if not more, important (e.g. Callimachus).

2. Modern Catullus. This Catullus, a self-conscious moderniser, derived his inspiration chiefly (or, in some versions, solely) from the Hellenistic poets, especially Callimachus. But he was able to transcend them, injecting life into 'dull' Alexandrian pedantry: 'He avoids', wrote A.M. Duff in the 1949 *Oxford Classical Dictionary*, 'the worst Alexandrian faults: obscurity, over-cleverness, excess of erudition, and allusiveness'. At the same time he also transcended his Roman predecessors, who had produced only crude works (the argument goes) in 'low' genres such as satire and mime.

The skill of this Catullus is best seen in some of the polymetrics and in the long poems. He is ingenious, so it must be assumed that he himself, not an editor, arranged the poems into their present order. Like Romantic Catullus, Modern Catullus stands aloof from the mainstream of first-century BC Roman culture – not because he is uniquely sensitive, but because he writes for a coterie of rarefied intellectuals. 'Modern' with a capital 'M', he is an ancient prototype of the Modernist poets T.S. Eliot or Ezra Pound (Peter Whigham, who translated Catullus in the 1960s, rendered poem 64 in a style close to that of Pound's *Cantos*).

This notion of Catullus also has several obvious pitfalls (made more obvious by my rhetoric above). Catullus' Roman forebears are downplayed in favour of his Greek sources. The long poems are given too much weight, and so are those of the polymetrics that display characteristically 'Modern' qualities, such as paradox, antithesis and vivid imagery. (So poem 11, which represents Catullus' wounded masculinity as a crushed flower, is a Modern favourite.) The view that Catullus was an out-and-out cultural elitist does not square with the frankly earthy aspect of his work – the obscenity, the slang, the debt to 'low' genres such as mime.

3. Roman Catullus. The most recent manifestation of Catullus in readers' imaginations, Roman Catullus seems, in many respects, the polar opposite of 'Catullus the Modern'. He participates fully and enthusiastically in his society and its mainstream culture. He jockeys for social superiority with friends and rivals at dinner parties (poems 12 and 13), and publicly dallies with prostitutes (poems 10 and 55). His posture is one of uncomplicated machismo. With his violent rages, sorrows and desires, this Catullus assembles his self from the stock characters of Roman New Comedy – the clever slaves, lovesick young men and angry fathers who appear in plays by Terence and Plautus. On this view, Catullus' savage iambics hark back to the work of Rome's first satirists, Ennius and Lucilius, while poems 34 and 63, both of which concern revered deities, are performance-pieces written for the religious festivals of Diana and the Megalesia (a festival in honour of Cybele).

While Modern Catullus is overly elitist and 'too clever by half', Roman Catullus, with his obsessive interest in his own and others' bodily appetites, is less self-consciously intellectual than we could reasonably expect of the author of poem 64. Indeed, it is this failure to account for the long poems which is Roman Catullus' most glaring deficiency. Nevertheless, this persona has usefully focused our attention on the Roman world to which Catullus belonged, whatever his precise role in it was.

*

1. Between Myth and History: The Life of Catullus

It is impossible to read a text without forming *some* idea of its author. Since this is an integral part of the reading process, I do not suggest that it is wrong to subscribe to this or that view of Catullus. But falling into the easy habit of imagining Catullus in a specific way can hinder interpretation. Readers embarking on the opening sequence of Catullus' poems should be alert to Catullus' own characterisation of his work, pre-eminently in poem 1. For as the next chapter demonstrates, the poet himself had clear ideas about how he wanted to appear in the eyes of his readers.

A note on the order of the poems

Perhaps the most debated issue in Catullus studies is the question of who arranged the poems into their present order. What has come down to us in our three medieval manuscripts (all copies of the single manuscript allegedly found at the bottom of a wine-barrel), after much winnowing and emending by editors, falls into three parts.

Poems 1-60, the 'polymetrics', are composed in a variety of metres (Greek *poly* means 'many'). These poems address myriad persons and subjects, and display a wide range of tones. Though rather a hodgepodge, they do seem to constitute a discrete part of the collection. Their total number of verses is 848, about enough to fill a single roll of papyrus (ancient Roman 'books' were in fact scrolls). Poems 18, 19, and 20, known as the 'Priapeia' after the Greek fertility god they honour, have been judged not to be Catullus' work and are excluded from modern editions, so that there is a jump between poem 17 and poem 21.

With poem 61, a 228-line marriage hymn, a new series of longer poems begins. It includes another marriage hymn (62); an account of the exotic myth of Attis and Cybele (63); an intricate 'little epic' on another myth, the marriage of Peleus and

Thetis (64); a verse letter in which the poet laments his brother's death and the difficulty of writing since (65); a poem narrated by a lock of hair belonging to the Hellenistic princess/queen Berenice (66); a poem in which a house-door recounts some scandals involving the mistress of the house (67); a second verse letter on the poet's grief at his brother's death (68A); and, possibly paired with this last piece, a letter of thanks to a friend named Allius, who has allowed Catullus and his mistress to meet secretly in his house (68B).

Yet the metre of poems 65-68 is elegiac couplets, the same metre as all the poems in the final section of the book. Consequently some critics argue that these three (or four) poems belong with 69-116 rather than the preceding group. They make a strong case, but most readers still find it natural to take 65-68 with 61-64. However, poems 61-68B add up to a somewhat unwieldy 1161 lines, while poems 61-64 total 795 lines, a length comparable to that of the polymetrics.

Most of the poems in the group 69-116 – the 'elegiacs' – consist of eight or fewer lines, and all of them are composed in elegiac couplets. (Not 'elegiac' strictly in the sense of 'mournful'. Although the metre was originally used for funeral songs, by Catullus' time it had begun to be used in a wide range of poetry.) Among the elegiacs are several Lesbia poems and nearly two dozen pieces of invective, many directed against Caesar's chief engineer Mamurra, or against a man named Gellius whose depravity the poet condemns. Taken together, the poems in this section are more obscene and abusive in character than the rest of the corpus, though there are a few notable exceptions, such as poem 101.

Who was responsible for this arrangement? Many scholars argue that Catullus himself was, on the evidence of poem 1, which is indisputably a dedication poem introducing a collection of poems. The problem is exactly which collection 1 introduces – the whole corpus of Catullus? Or only part of it, perhaps poems 1-60? Martial, the first-century AD epigrammatist, compares his patron Stella's *Dove* – presumably a book of poems – to the *Sparrow* (*Passer*) of Catullus. His remark implies that a number of Catullus' poems, whether ten or sixty, could have stood apart as a separate collection under the title *Passer* in antiquity. Indeed, in poem 1 Catullus refers to his poetry book as a *libellus*, a 'little book'; totalling nearly 2,300 verses, the entire corpus hardly would have qualified as 'little'. So, one argument goes, Catullus must have arranged and published three *libelli* in his lifetime, and later the papyrus scrolls were printed together in book format. (Standing between the two camps, Kenneth Quinn has argued that 1-60 were published by Catullus, while the 'scrappier and shorter' 69-116 were compiled by a later editor.)

Dissenters from this view point out that there are no references to Books I, II and III of Catullus in the works of the ancient grammarians (who often quoted 'snippets' of Greek and Latin literature). I myself see no absolutely compelling evidence either for or against Catullus' editorship. Unfortunately, since the poetry collections of Catullus' fellow neoterics have not survived, we will probably never know what principles they followed when arranging their poems into books.

Defining Catullan Poetics: The Opening Sequence

Poem 1 - dedication

Whether his published book included poems 1-60 or 1-116, Catullus fully exploits the programmatic potential of its first piece. In poem 1 he dedicates his new book to his friend Cornelius (the biographer/historian Cornelius Nepos). For attentive readers, though, he also provides important clues amounting to a 'crash course' in Catullan poetics (1.1-4):

> To whom do I give a smart new little book
> Just polished off with dry pumice?
> To you, Cornelius; for you've always
> Regarded my trifles as *something*.

Into these first four lines, Catullus packs several meaningful words that advertise his poetic ideals. In fact, he gets three into the very first line, characterising the book we're reading as 'smart' and 'new', and dubbing it a 'booklet' or 'little book'. The Latin word he uses here for 'smart', *lepidus*, was something of a vogue-word in the mid-first century BC, its meaning not far from English 'stylish' or 'sleek', or indeed British-English 'smart'. To cultured Romans, whatever was *lepidus* was the polar opposite of what was rustic, awkward, or plodding.

'New' and 'little' may seem to be very commonplace terms,

but both had a special significance for the neoteric writers. 'New', *novus*, conveys at least two meanings in line 1: first, the physical book Catullus gives to Cornelius is 'new' in that the papyrus roll has just been copied and polished; at the same time, the poems themselves are new – and representative of an emerging poetic voice or style (hence the label *poetae novi*, 'new poets'). *Libellus* ('little book') is a diminutive form of *liber* (book). Such diminutives appear with great frequency in neoteric verse in general, and in Catullus' polymetrics particularly,[1] connoting as they do both a certain delicacy and the ease of intimate conversation.

Moreover, the term *libellus* can also be related to the Alexandrian disdain for epic and other large-scale genres in favour of shorter poetry. 'I hate the cyclic poem', Callimachus (third century BC) declares in one of his epigrams, 'nor do I take pleasure in the road that bears many back and forth' (*Epigrams* 30). Elsewhere, in the prologue to his poem *Aetia* (*Origins*), Callimachus writes that the god Apollo had ordered him, 'Feed the [sacrificial] victim ... but keep the Muse slender' (23-4); the implication is that although long-winded poems may be popular with the crowds, Callimachus seeks a different – more select – audience.

'Polished' and 'dry' in line 2 may also have literary connotations, the former connoting a smooth or polished style as well as a polished-off papyrus scroll, the latter suggesting, perhaps, the dry hours of study that have gone into the book. Also significant is Catullus' use of the word 'trifles', *nugae*. He has told us his book is smart, new, slender and polished – does he sincerely believe that the poems are mere trifles? Balancing *nugae* against the descriptive terms used in lines 1 and 2, it seems likely that Catullus is being self-deprecating.

The remainder of poem 1 (5-10) speaks of Cornelius' bold

and unique literary achievement, but is rather more vague about the book at hand:

> Even when you dared, the only Italian,
> To unfurl the whole past in three scrolls
> (They're learned, by Jupiter, and laborious).
> So have this booklet here, for what it's worth,
> Which, O Maiden Patron,
> May you keep fresh beyond one lifetime.

Cornelius has set down the whole of history in only three papyrus rolls – almost certainly Nepos' lost *Chronicle*. This is an achievement substantially different, of course, from Catullus' 'trifles' (though if Catullus lived to see the publication of his complete collection, then 'three scrolls' in line 6 may be an allusion to the tripartite structure of his own corpus). Catullus goes on to tell us that his friend's history is erudite and 'laborious'. Does he mean 'laborious' in the sense of 'difficult to read', or 'difficult to write'? In the second sense, this would be a compliment, since Callimacheans took pride in their careful artistic efforts. The Latin word *laboriosus* is ambiguous, and so, perhaps, is Catullus' opinion of his friend's work.

'So have this booklet here, for what it's worth', the poet offers in line 8. Colloquial words, most of them pronouns, predominate in lines 8 and 9: 'this booklet here', *quidquid hoc libelli* (literally, 'whatever [part] of this book'); and 'for what it's worth', *qualecumque*. Looking back to line 4, we find another indefinite pronoun, 'something' (*aliquid*). The vague language Catullus employs here hints at modesty as well as a certain nonchalance. But that modesty is rendered false, it seems to me, by the more vivid adjectives of lines 1 and 2 – for although he pretends not to value his trifles, he has already called them smart and fresh.

This suspicion is confirmed in the poem's final verse. There, Catullus prays that his 'Maiden Patron', or Muse, will make sure his poems outlast him. So much for indifferent trifles – clearly, Catullus expects these poems to bring him lasting fame.

Nor is the invocation to the Muse an empty formula. It conveys the important detail that Catullus is not dependent on a *mortal* patron. Lucretius, an older contemporary of Catullus, dedicated his Epicurean masterpiece *On the Nature of Things* to Memmius (the same Memmius denounced by Catullus, in fact); later Horace dedicated the first three books of his *Odes* to his patron Maecenas. Catullus, apparently, does not have to please a powerful man like Maecenas or Memmius. Presumably his social status is high enough that he is free to offer his poetry book to a peer, Cornelius (who like Catullus is 'of the Italians', i.e. provincial, and not from a leading Roman family).

The shift of address from Cornelius to the Muse at line 9, besides underscoring Catullus' social status, also raises a puzzling question: does Catullus really dedicate his book to Cornelius, or does he ultimately withhold it from him, presenting it to the Muse instead? In my view, the question is better left unanswered. With its skilfully deployed ambiguity, poem 1 makes us want to find out whether Catullus' poems are indeed trifles, and if they are, whether they still surpass weightier works like Cornelius' history. It makes us suspect, and hope, that the poet's modesty is false, and that his trifles are, to use Catullus' own optimistic term, *something*.

Poems 2 and 3 – 'the sparrow poems'

Catullus makes good on his promise of 'trifles' immediately, in the first line of poem 2: 'Sparrow, my girl's delight'. The poem is so trifling as to address a bird – the pet sparrow of the poet's girlfriend. Catullus' reference to his *puella* (girlfriend or mistress) is our first hint that romantic love will be one of his themes. Though the sparrow is ostensibly the subject of this poem, from line 2 onwards it is consigned to a secondary role as the object of the girl's games. Those games are described in lines 2-4, where a string of verbs vividly evokes her hand-gestures (my italics):

> Whom she always *plays with*, whom she *cuddles* in her lap,
> To whose eagerness she *offers up* her fingertips
> And *provokes* sharp bites

Play with; cuddle; offer up; provoke – surely it's not far-fetched to say that the girl is playing a kind of love-game with her sparrow. This interpretation is supported by 'delight' in line 1; the Latin word in the original, *deliciae*, ranges in meaning from 'delight(s)' to 'favourite' (as in a favourite pet) to 'naughty things', and has erotic overtones.

Catullus, then, is establishing an unusual love triangle. His love-object is the girl ('my girl', he calls her in line 1), and yet the girl's 'delight' is her pet bird, whom she teases and caresses as she might a lover. In the middle section of the poem (5-8), the dynamics of the love-triangle become clearer:

> When it gratifies my flushed desire
> To play some sweet game,
> a little solace for her hurt,
> I think, so her heavy passion can rest:

Significantly, the poet describes his beloved in line 5 as 'my flushed desire' – his seeking-after, his *own* longing. In other words, he seems to assimilate the object of his love to the emotion of love itself. This striking synecdoche (desire [for the girl] = the desired girl) points up the fact that Catullus hasn't entirely won his girl yet; she is longed for, but not quite attained.[2] And she, we learn in line 7, toys with her bird to assuage her 'hurt' – the emotional pain of nursing her 'heavy' (unconsummated?) passion. She displaces her desire for the poet (or for someone else) onto the sparrow, enjoying a vicarious intimacy with her beloved this way.

With the hesitant 'I think' of line 8, the pace slows as Catullus turns from description to speculation about the motive underlying the girl's game: he suggests that it helps to ease the intensity of her passion. The poet wishes he could find relief in it, too (9-10; 2B 1-3):

> That I could play with you as she does
> And lift the sad cares from my mind!
> [It is as welcome to me as they say
> To the swift-footed girl was the golden apple
> That loosened her girdle, long tied.]

Catullus' 'sad cares' sound more serious than the girl's 'heavy passion', which leads some readers to interpret his wish as a rueful one: even if he played with the bird, it would be no use against *his* troubles. One might conclude that Catullus' 'cares' are those of a discouraged or spurned lover, and perhaps that his description of the girl's ardour as 'heavy' is ironic.

Is the *puella* of poem 2 the fickle Lesbia? This interpretation fits well with other of Catullus' poems that concern his affair with Lesbia and her betrayals – but the girl in this poem is never identified. All sorts of readings are possible: the girl *is* Lesbia and her passion really *is* 'heavy'; or Catullus' 'cares' spring, not from any betrayal by her, but from her absence; or – the girl is not

Lesbia, and Catullus' 'cares' are not even love-related. Like poem 85 (discussed in the Introduction), poem 2 demonstrates how difficult it can be to read a Catullus poem without mining the rest of the corpus for explanatory details.

Lines 11-13 ('It is as welcome to me ...'), ever since the editor Battista Guarino looked askance on them in the early sixteenth century, have been isolated from poem 2 proper and have hovered, a baffling fragment, between poems 2 and 3. In them Catullus compares himself to the mythical virgin Atalanta, who had promised to marry any man who could beat her in a foot-race; eventually one of her suitors, Hippomenes, succeeded by dropping golden apples in her path, which she stopped to pick up. (The comparison of himself to a female figure is not unusual for Catullus, we shall see; see the discussions of poems 11, 51 and 68B below.) Critic William Fitzgerald, who makes a persuasive case that the three lines belong with the preceding poem, also clarifies the relevance of Catullus' allusion to Atalanta: 'At the end of the poem', Fitzgerald writes, 'we are told that Lesbia's game with the sparrow is itself the consummation to be desired: it would be as pleasing to Catullus as the apple that brought the end of virginity to Atalanta ... the game that suggested sex now becomes its alternative or substitute.'[3]

Poem 2, then – whether it deals with an episode in the 'Lesbia affair' or not – by uniting playfulness and eroticism (*deliciae*), signals that both will be important features of Catullus' style. Poem 2 is itself a love-game, like the one it describes; Catullus' wish that he could play with the sparrow is a form of flirtation, a textual come-on to his girl (and, indirectly, to his reader).

Poem 3 is no less playful, though now the girl's game has ended – her sparrow has died. Written in the mode of an ancient Greek dirge, the poem begins with an invocation (1-5):

2. Defining Catullan Poetics: The Opening Sequence

Weep, O Venuses and Cupids
And everyone who's charming:
My girlfriend's sparrow is dead –
Sparrow, my girl's delight,
Whom she loved more than her own eyes.

'Venuses and Cupids' and 'everyone who's charming' are a far cry from the powerful gods or patrons whom ancient authors typically hailed in lofty genres such as epic. Lucretius, for example, invokes the goddess Venus in the opening of his epic 'On the Nature of Things'. He reverently conjures the goddess as mighty and life-giving; whereas Catullus' plural 'Venuses and Cupids', on the other hand, seem less imposing, bringing to mind mythological nymphs or graces. (The expression 'Venuses and Cupids' may have been proverbial in Catullus' Rome.) Catullus also puns on the goddess' name here, drawing out an alternative meaning of the Latin word *venus* – the abstraction 'charm' or 'love', with its cognate adjective *venustus*, 'charming'. The gap between the solemn conventions of the elegiac mode and Catullus' light tone and trifling theme – the death of a girl's pet bird – make poem 3 a mock-elegy.

The poet's summons to 'everyone who's charming' to attend his words is simultaneously a playful dare and a compliment. It prompts us to ask ourselves – does this description apply to us? And, if we read on, will we learn what it is that Catullus considers charming? Clearly, though, Catullus would not call on 'everyone who's charming' unless he assumed that a good many of his readers qualified. In this sense, it's a compliment – to us and to himself too, for the poet also must be charming to enjoy such a readership.

In the remainder of poem 3, we see Catullan charm emerge as a quality combining daintiness and wit, and tinged with sex appeal. It is never explicitly defined; rather, the poet offers us verbal clues to it – singular words that flash out and invite our admiration. These words are mainly diminutives, slang or dialect words, and neologisms (coinages). They ought to be savoured in the original Latin, replete with soft 'l' and 'r' sounds: *mellitus*, 'honeyed' (6, describing the sparrow); *pipiabat*, 'he [the sparrow] kept chirping' (10; the only appearance of this onomatopoeic word in classical Latin texts); *tenebricosum*, 'shady little' (11; facetiously applied to the road that leads to the underworld); *miselle*, 'poor little' (16; used of the dead sparrow); *turgiduli*, 'swollen little' (18; used of the crying girl's eyes). This last usage is, to my mind, the most provocative; the playful term may come off as belittling or cold, a charm*less* aestheticising of the girl's grief.

Catullus is challenging us to enjoy his pretty miniatures, and to adopt his pose of amused detachment when confronted with excessive emotion (as displayed by the weeping girl). Most of us will want to enter into the spirit of Catullus' literary game, not minding too much that our admittance into the circle of charming people (*venustiores*) is really his doing, not ours.

Poems 5, 7 and 48: Catullus' kisses

There is not space in this volume to consider all 116 of Catullus' poems, or even half of them. Therefore it will be necessary to isolate the most representative, most intriguing texts for discussion; but not in a way that they seem devoid of context. To present selected poems in strict numerical order (for example, 4, 7, 11, 15 …) is not an ideal solution, for Catullus' poems are not arranged chronologically. In fact – besides the basic three-part division – his poems have no discernible pattern of arrangement. At the same time neighbouring poems often do form a pair (like 2 and 3 above), and there is too much thematic overlap to categorise poems easily into groups of 'love poems', 'satiric poems', and so forth. Moreover, poems addressing the same person tend not to appear side by side.

The strategy I employ below is to identify 'clusters' of related poems from different parts of the corpus, while broadly following numerical order. Though no doubt somewhat arbitrary, these clusters are intended to illustrate key aspects of Catullus' work. Within each cluster the individual poems shed light on one another – as do poems 5, 7 and 48, the 'kiss poems'.

*

Poem 5 is one of Catullus' most famous, having spawned scores of English imitations over the past four hundred years. One of the earliest and finest of these versions is by Thomas Campion, whose alliterative rendering of the first line has since become standard: 'Let us live, Lesbia, and let us love'. (Note that this is the first time the name 'Lesbia' appears in the collection, even though many readers automatically associate the sparrow poems with her.)

And the urgency of Catullus' tone still sweeps readers up into his passion (1-6):

> Let us live, Lesbia, and let us love,
> And as for all the gripes of stodgy old men,
> Let's assess them at one cent.
> Suns can set and rise again
> But for us, when brief light has dimmed,
> There's one endless night to sleep.

Catullus tries to persuade Lesbia that they should disregard the grumbling of old men (representatives of old-fashioned Roman morals), and live as they wish – that is, together. In lines 1-3, the first-person plural verbs *vivamus* ('let us live'), *amemus* ('let us love') and *aestimemus* ('let us assess'), besides lending rhetorical force, insist on the unity of the lovers and stress the distinction between them and the rest of society.

Line 4, however, brings a transition to the third-person voice and an abruptly dispassionate tone. Lines 4-6 constitute a somber aphorism on the brevity of human life in the face of nature's eternity; this belies any impression we might have had that the poem is an unpremeditated confession, that Catullus is speaking strictly 'from the heart'. (The aphorism is so impersonal and un-trifling, in fact, that it became a popular moral *sententia* – a piece of proverbial wisdom – during the Renaissance.) Rhetorically, the shift in voice and tone from lines 1-3 to lines 4-6 is very effective. It catches us by surprise, and makes the juxtaposed three-line units seem to stand out from each other in relief.

A second major shift occurs at line 7, when Catullus' reflection on mortality suddenly becomes a demand that Lesbia kiss him, and kiss him again ...

> Give me a thousand kisses, then a hundred –
> Then another thousand, then a second hundred –
> Then yet another thousand, then a hundred.
> Then, when we've amassed many thousands of kisses
> We'll muddle the accounts, so even we won't know,
> And so no enemy should begrudge us
> When he learns how many kisses we've got.

As many commentators have pointed out, Catullus employs the vocabulary of the accountant here, totting up hundreds and thousands of kisses before vowing ultimately to 'muddle the accounts'. This verb, *conturbare*, was often used of money-counting by the Romans. Moreover, *da mi* ('Give me …') may have been a common Latin formula for introducing financial transactions.

So, following the initial opposition set up between 'us' (lovers) and 'them' (old men, or moral conventions) comes another, between the world of *negotium* (business) and the world of *amor* (love) – which, many would argue, is simply not subject to computation. Because of this, it is easy to read the poem as a gesture of romantic rebellion. '[Catullus] mimics the world he scorns and must inhabit', writes John Henderson in an essay on the kiss poems. Yet as Henderson perceives, the poet is not wholly in earnest. 'He is … sending up seriousness by what he counts, and makes us count', Henderson continues. 'Kisses, indeed! Could a poet make more serious mischief?'[4]

As Henderson observes, poem 5, like the sparrow poems, enacts a game – a love-game that is also a numbers-game, and vice versa. This game makes the most sense if we locate it in a public setting. Perhaps Catullus and Lesbia are stealing kisses from under the noses of 'stodgy old men', and keeping count as they go.

In the second of the kiss poems, Lesbia has asked Catullus just how many kisses will satisfy him. Slyly, Catullus replies (3-8):

As many as the grains of Libyssan sand
That lie in silphium-sprouting Cyrene
Between the oracle of sweltering Jove
And venerable Battus' holy sepulchre –
Or as many as the stars that, when night is silent,
Watch the stolen loves of mortals.

This is a clever variation on the number-game of poem 5, a trick designed to sidestep numbers altogether. Ostensibly, Catullus answers Lesbia's question, but the 'sums' he offers are – paradoxically – innumerable, the sum of stars in the night sky and the total sand on the North African coast. 'Silphium-sprouting Cyrene' (silphium was a fennel-like African plant) and 'venerable Battus' holy sepulchre' are obscure allusions to Cyrene, an exotic outpost of Rome in modern-day Libya and the birthplace of Callimachus (who was said to be descended from Cyrene's legendary founder, Battus). By means of such place-name-dropping, Catullus pays honour to a literary exemplar, and playfully extends his game of evasion.

Although it is not so well known as 5 or 7 and appears near the end of the polymetrics, a third poem, 48, is where the ideals of the kiss poems and sparrow poems coalesce. Again, Catullus writes of kisses and wildly incalculable numbers:

> Your honey-eyes, Juventius,
> If someone let me keep kissing them,
> I'd keep kissing three hundred thousand times
> But never feel I could be satisfied,
> Not if the harvest of our kissing
> Was packed closer than dried corn.

Continuing the number-games of 5 and 7, Catullus dreams of lavishing on Juventius three hundred thousand kisses: the sum is ludicrous in its sheer size and its arbitrariness (why not two hundred thousand, or four hundred thousand?). To equate these kisses with a dense crop of corn-ears is witty, for it shows up the disparity between what is small, intimate and beyond the reach of numbers (a kiss), on the one hand, and what is large, impersonal and endlessly inventoried – a farmer's corn crop – on the other. Catullus' metaphor is vivid and curiously appropriate. Kissing and eating are not so dissimilar. Why shouldn't kisses put one in mind of food – whether corn or Juventius' 'honey-eyes'? In poem 48, as in 7 and 5, Catullus' ecstasy of kissing bursts the bounds of *negotium*. Instead of being defined by the world of numbers, it subsumes that world, leaving us with the impression of kisses more natural and plentiful than the harvest itself.

Poem 48 is no less artistically successful than its close counterpart 7, but it has not received nearly as much attention. The reason lies with its addressee: 'Juventius' is, of course, a masculine name. In Rome, citizen men commonly initiated sexual relationships with adolescent boys, though they usually shunned the 'passive' role, which was judged effeminate. (For more on Roman attitudes to sexuality, see the next chapter and Chapter 7.) It seems reasonable to conclude that Juventius was Catullus' boy-lover, probably a slave.

If at any point we took poems 2, 3, 5 and 7 as proof that Catullan *amor* is exclusive and heterosexual, we were misguided. Poem 48 has so much in common with these others that it certainly should be grouped with them. Catullus even uses the same word, 'honeyed', of his girlfriend's sparrow (poem 3) and of Juventius' eyes (poem 48), blurring together heterosexual and homosexual love. Catullus' homosexual poems – a dozen or so in total, including another, 99, addressed to Juventius – have long provoked anxiety, borne out by the number of translations of poem 48 that represent Juventius as a young woman. (Even Byron addressed his version 'To Ellen'). In recent years, however, there has been a new effort to consider sexuality in Catullus' work in light of Roman ideas about sex and gender, which differed markedly from those of modern Western societies. The next chapter examines Catullus' poems to his male friends, and their blend of camaraderie, competition and sexual desire.

Male Friendship in Catullus

Poems 11, 15 and 16: Furius, Aurelius, Catullus

Catullus addresses the same two men, Furius and Aurelius, in poems 11 and 16; the latter is also the sole addressee of poem 15. All we know of the historical Furius and Aurelius is that they were Catullus' friends. However, the relationship shared by the three men (at least as Catullus describes it) is not what modern readers would consider typical of friends. Catullan friendship encompasses a wide range of attitudes and emotions: sexual desire, suspicion, possessiveness, anger, vulnerability and dependency. A steady and warm regard for one's friend (what today we might call 'emotional support'), by contrast, does not seem to be particularly valued, and often gets crowded out by more unruly emotions.

Poem 11 begins with a direct apostrophe to Furius and Aurelius, whom the poet identifies simply as his 'companions'. The Latin noun used here, *comites*, had associations with the Roman empire and its government: Cicero used it to denote the group of men who accompanied a senior magistrate into a foreign province. This sense of *'travelling* companion' is certainly brought into play in the first three stanzas of poem 11, an evocative chronicle of distant lands which Catullus proposes to visit. 'Whether he will venture into the outermost lands of the Indians … or to Hyrcanian, or luxurious Arabian places, or to those of the Scythians, or the arrow-wielding Parthians …' (1; 5-6). Compass-like, Catullus traces the limit of the known world, moving roughly from East to West, from India to the Middle East – Arabia, Hyrcania, Sacia and Parthia (the last three are in present-day Iran) – on to Egypt, then finally up to Gaul and the northern frontier of Rome's empire, Britain.

What purpose does this epic-style catalogue serve? Its function is twofold: first, it demonstrates the loyalty of Furius and Aurelius to their companion Catullus. The poet asserts that he will make his way into remote territories; although his precise destination is uncertain, the intention to set out is expressed with confidence (*penetrabit* in line 2, 'he *will* penetrate into', is more assured than the subjunctive 'he *may* [or *might*] penetrate into'). Catullus will embark on a journey, and Furius and Aurelius are, he trusts, 'prepared to venture' (14) to the ends of the earth with him.

Secondly, the catalogue brings into focus the places on the margins of the Roman world, and prepares us for the figurative marginalisation that occurs next, in lines 13-24. For in the second half of the poem Catullus finds himself displaced, though not geographically:

All these places, whatever heaven's will
Should bring, you're prepared to brave –
Convey to my girl a few
Not kind words:

May she be happy and healthy with her adulterers,
Whom she smothers, three hundred together, in her embrace
Loving none truly, but again and again
Crushing all their loins;

And may she not as before count on my love,
Which by her fault has crumpled like a flower
On the verge of a meadow, when it's been
Nicked by a passing plough.

46

Catullus does not ask his friends to accompany him to a far-flung land, but to give his girlfriend a brief message – literally, 'a few (not good) words' (15-16). With this pointed understatement, the mood shifts to bitter disgust, and then finally to pathos. The mock-serious hyperbole of the first three stanzas (will they *really* venture so far?) reappears in lines 18-20, but this time the effect is grotesque: Catullus' girlfriend holds three hundred men together in her monstrous embrace, repeatedly 'breaking open [their] groins' (*ilia rumpens*). Without using any obscenities – or even *because* he avoids them – Catullus conveys to us a sense of the extraordinary sexual violence this woman (or his demonised image of her) wreaks.

The final stanza of poem 11 brings about a breathtaking finish, with Catullus comparing his love for the girl to a flower at the edge of a meadow, clipped by a passing plough. The vulnerability of this flower could not differ more starkly from the easy confidence with which Catullus mentally roamed the world in the poem's first half. There the verb he used, *penetrare*, has sexual connotations (which are clear from its English derivative); the flower simile in the last stanza has equally plain but very different sexual connotations, of 'plucked' virginity. A possible precedent for Catullus' imagery is a lyric fragment by Sappho (fr. 105b), describing a crushed hyacinth. Originally part of a wedding poem, it probably went on to compare the hyacinth to the bride's lost innocence:

Like the hyacinth which shepherds tread underfoot in the mountains, and on the ground the purple flower ... (translated by David A. Campbell)[1]

Catullus' regard for Sappho, who wrote almost six hundred years before him, is apparent from his imitation of Sapphic themes and of the lyric stanza named after her, in his poems 61, 62 and most notably 51. So for him to adapt this simile from Sappho is not surprising, though what he applies it to – a man's passion, as opposed to a girl's chastity – is.

There is a significant parallel in Catullus' poem between the flower's location at the edge of the meadow and the margins of empire referred to earlier; the same adjective, *ultimus*, 'remotest' or 'farthest', is used of both. In other words, the poet aligns himself with what is peripheral. His flower-like helplessness and evident sympathy for non- (or barely-) Roman peoples may be interpreted as a challenge to orthodox values. In Catullus' Rome, one's civic identity and manhood depended on each other: the lesser the Roman, the lesser the man. So the poet's picture of himself in poem 11 was radically unconventional, as David Konstan remarks:

> [Catullus] simply exists at the boundary, like the populations defeated by Rome's legions, where Lesbia's violence has found and destroyed him. Catullus' self-presentation in this poem is the product of his own marginalisation, as he perceives it, in regard to the Roman center of power …. He projects an alternative vision of love and simultaneously casts himself as the victim of an inexorable system.[2]

What does poem 11 tell us about Catullus' friendship with Furius and Aurelius? A reader might reach two near-contradictory conclusions: on the one hand, the poet trusts his friends enough to admit to them that his is the weaker position in the love-affair, a humiliating confession for any well-born Roman man; at the same time, he defines his friendship with Furius and Aurelius *against* his love for his girlfriend, with the subtle implication that his male friendships must compete with the love-affair.

3. Male Friendship in Catullus

Eve Kosofsky Sedgwick, in her influential book *Between Men: English Literature and Male Homosocial Desire*, observes that the erotic relationships in many literary texts can be mapped onto a triangle. Two of the triangle's 'points' normally represent men's roles, while the third is frequently a woman's. From point to point there runs a continual negotiation for control, which may take various forms: the men may compete for the woman's love, for example, or together they might denounce her. Sedgwick further observes that, in the texts she studies, 'male bonding' often depends on a mutual rejection of the woman or women in general, and includes an element – sometimes very marked – of homoeroticism. It will be helpful to bear Sedgwick's ideas in mind when considering Catullus' numerous homoerotic poems.

Poem 11 represents friendship as characterised by mutual dependence, both in physically risky circumstances and in emotionally treacherous dealings with women. Catullus' trust in Furius and Aurelius – his confidence that they would follow him anywhere – is contrasted against Lesbia's ungrateful presumption on him. Of this he bitterly cautions, 'may she not as before count on my love'.

A similar 'erotic triangle' provides the framework for poem 15. With the seven words of this poem's first sentence, the triangle's three 'points' are fixed: 'I entrust *myself* and *my beloved* to you,/ *Aurelius*' (1-2). Much like that in poem 11, this triangle consists of Catullus, his friend (only one here) and his lover (*meos amores*, literally 'my loves', though interestingly *amores* can mean love *poems*, too). Lines 2-5 establish the three-way dynamics. Catullus asks Aurelius a 'modest favour' (2) – that 'you [Aurelius] will watch over the boy for me modestly' (5). So this triangle differs from poem 11's in that it is entirely male. As in 11, however, Catullus' position seems to be one of relative weakness. Reluctantly, he must yield control over his boy-lover to Aurelius, and can only beseech his friend to take responsibility for the boy.

The balance of power tilts further towards Aurelius when Catullus admits that he fears, not the intentions of the public at large, but (9-13)

> In fact it's you I fear, and your penis,
> Which endangers both good boys and bad.
> Foist it wherever, however you please,
> At any opportunity – somewhere else,
> I'm just making one modest (I think) exception.

As at 11.18, where the poet's girlfriend is said to embrace three hundred men at the same time, Catullus puts exaggerated language to grotesque (and comic) effect here, describing Aurelius' penis almost as if it were detached from the rest of his body. It is a menacing instrument, which Aurelius tends to 'foist' indiscriminately (a policeman's truncheon comes to mind). And the poet urges him to continue to do so, with a single 'modest' exception – his own boy-lover.

The concept of modesty is integral to poem 15. Latin *pudor*, 'modesty' or 'shame', and the related word *pudicitia*, 'chastity' (sometimes a feminine personification, like 'Lady Justice'), were fundamental values in Roman society. Virtuous Roman matrons were expected to embody *pudicitia*, while those women who transgressed social norms were rebuked as *impudens*, brazen. Although *pudor* and especially *pudicitia* were commonly associated with feminine virtue, the terms could also connote pious modesty in men. Hence Cicero invoked *pudicitia* as a quintessentially Roman, but not male or female, quality, in one of his orations against the conspirator Catiline (*Against Catiline* 2.25).

Pudens is how the poet describes his own request to Aurelius;

the favour he seeks is that Aurelius, in turn, conduct himself *pudice*, modestly. For Catullus to associate his pederastic behaviour with *pudor* would have raised a few eyebrows among his contemporaries. It was not objectionable in ancient Rome for men to have sex with boys (provided that the boys were slaves and the men were free citizens, and took the active role in intercourse), but to have sex promiscuously (with boys especially) was frowned upon as a token of a very undesirable quality, *incontinentia*, the failure to restrain one's baser urges. Clearly, then, Catullus' use of the term *pudor* and its cognates in poem 15 has an ironic bite.

At the opposite end of the Roman moral spectrum from *pudor* are *scelus*, 'crime', and *culpa*, 'mistake', both of which, Catullus says in 15, Aurelius will have committed if – in a fit of madness (*furor*), another un-Roman concept – he corrupts the boy. If Catullus should find Aurelius guilty, he promises to deliver a hair-raising punishment (17-19):

> Oh, then you'll be made miserable by your cruel fate,
> When – legs spread apart, backdoor open –
> Radishes and mullets ramrod you!

Forcefully – to say the least – Catullus asserts himself as the dominant third of the poem's erotic triangle. There is a clear correspondence between his violent rhetoric and the act of physical violence he threatens: to penetrate another man was a sign of one's masculinity in Rome, while to submit to penetration was seen as humiliating. And though the penalty Catullus describes seems outrageous, it was a known, though rare, form of punishment for adulterers; the poet Juvenal (AD *c.* 50 – *c.* 127) describes an angry husband using mullets to revenge himself on his wife's lover (*Satires* 10.314-17). This lends a twist to the poem's shocking conclusion. Catullus would penalise the person who violated his pederastic liaison exactly as if it were a legal, heterosexual marriage – a nonsensical, perhaps impious equation, to Roman eyes.

Should we take Catullus' threat seriously? His repeated ironic use of *pudor* and related words suggests not. More likely this kind of macho posturing was simply one aspect of Catullus' friendship with Aurelius; it seems to have been common to male friendships in their society. Another factor in Catullus and Aurelius' friendship was, evidently, the sharing of a boy-lover (or multiple boy-lovers). This presents a contrast to poem 11, in which Catullus, Aurelius and Furius mutually *reject* Catullus' girlfriend. In poem 15, although Catullus and Aurelius compete for the boy, they do so playfully; even the retribution the poet threatens is ludicrous, and maybe titillating, too.

Unlike 15, poem 16 does not gradually crescendo to a final rhetorical blast. It immediately launches into violent obscenity (1-6):

I'll ram you up your ass and in your mouth,
Aurelius you fag, Furius you pansy,
Who thought – because my little poems are soft –
That I'm not quite respectable.
The devoted poet himself ought to be proper;
His little poems don't have to be.

Here, as in the preceding poem, *pudor* is the critical issue. Aurelius and Furius have accused Catullus of being *parum pudicus* ('not quite respectable'), because he has written 'soft' verses. To disprove their accusation, and demonstrate his *pudor*, Catullus vows to inflict on them two stiff (if readers will excuse the pun) penalties: *pedicare* ('to penetrate [them] anally') and *irrumare* ('to penetrate orally').[3] In Western culture today, the idea that a man could prove he's not 'soft' (effeminate) by initiating sex with another man is paradoxical, but in ancient Rome – provided the initiator took the active role – it betokened virility.

However, what must have seemed comical – or possibly objectionable – to Catullus' contemporaries is the affiliation he implies between *pudicus* and *pedicare*. True, a 'modest' or upright Roman citizen might have physically attacked a thief who had stolen his goods, or an adulterer who had slept with his wife. (In theory at least – whether Roman men regularly exercised this legal right is doubtful.) But a friend who had made a mildly insulting remark? This is hardly conceivable. In fact, the poet's disproportionate threats lend credence to Aurelius and Furius' claim that he is 'not quite respectable'. Catullus, ironically, now seems very much like the *impudicus* Aurelius of poem 15. His actions, too, are guided by a single unclean (in the Roman view) part of his body, which he wields without restraint.

This extremely sexually aggressive Catullus is, as Amy Richlin argues, a version of the one figure who stands at the centre of all Roman sexual humour: the fertility god Priapus. Priapus' domain was the garden, and he meted out violent punishment to thieves he encountered there. The punishment was chiefly sexual in nature – not coincidentally, Priapus is depicted in ancient art with a huge, erect phallus. On Richlin's theory, the Catullus of poem 16, like Priapus, defends a bounded area (his 'soft' poetry) from those who would defile it.

In verses 5-6, Catullus attempts to draw a distinction between his personal morals and those of his poems, insisting that he is *pius* ('devoted') and *castus* ('proper') notwithstanding what he writes. His pithy self-defence was echoed by later Roman authors afraid that their characters would be judged by the raciness of their work. Ovid, after offending the emperor Augustus with 'a poem and an error', was sent into exile in 8 BC;

in his poem *Tristia* ('Melancholia') he draws a Catullan distinction between his life and his art (2.353-6):

> Believe me, my morals differ from my poetry
> (For my life is modest, but my Muse is jocose),
> And a large part of my work is disingenuous, made-up:
> It allows itself more liberties than its author.

In a similar vein (and perhaps with Ovid's unhappy fate in mind), Martial assured the emperor Domitian that 'my page is lascivious, my life upstanding' (*Epigrams* I.4.8).

In poem 16, as in poems 1 and 2, Catullus tries to guide our reading of his verse. Whereas at the beginning of the book he identified urbane charm and playfulness as the distinguishing features of his style, now he justifies his obscene rhetoric on aesthetic grounds: poetry can have 'salt and style' (*salem ac leporem*, 7) only when it's indecent. He would like us, he maintains, never to confuse his life with his art. Yet this stricture raises more questions than it answers. Are his Priapic threats merely rhetorical, or not? In lines 8-11, the 'respectable' poet seems to do an about-face, stating as one of his poetic aims the ability to rouse an 'itch' in an old man's loins. How literally should we interpret this? Surely a 'devoted' and 'proper' poet would not want to incite his readers to immodest acts? Or perhaps the revenge Catullus proposes *is* 'real'; that is, it is appropriate to his friends' crime after all. Because Furius and Aurelius mistake the softness of the poems for the character of the poet himself, Catullus apes their literal-mindedness, wilfully confusing hostile rhetoric with physical violence, obscene rhetoric with 'real' sex.

Already, from the evidence of these three poems, Catullan friendship seems bewilderingly complex. The poet initially has faith in his friends' abiding loyalty to him; he depends on their help in his troubled love-affair with his mistress. But in 15, he doubts that Aurelius will prove trustworthy, and threatens him with violence in case he shouldn't. Lastly, he hurls degrading insults at both friends and looks forward to a horrific revenge on them. Described thus, poems 11, 15 and 16 could be read as a chronological series, relating the gradual disillusionment of Catullus with his errant friends.

Yet the earnest tone, formal language and lyric metre of poem 11 set it apart from 15 and 16, which are composed in the more jaunty hendecasyllabic metre, and feature more colloquial diction including obscenities (absent from the higher genres of classical poetry, such as epic and tragedy, and also from poem 11). Thirty years ago, Kenneth Quinn attributed such discrepancies in tone and style to Catullus' having multiple 'levels of intent' – that is, he had high artistic aims for some poems, low ones for others. While it is certainly possible that Catullus had different, more ambitious intentions for 11 than he did for 15 and 16, this notion obscures the fact that all of Catullus' poems are well crafted, and that apparently 'low-intent' poems like 15 and 16 are far from simplistic.

Poems 11, 15 and 16 give ample demonstration of Catullus' rhetorical range, and of a concept of friendship as an ever-shifting, competitive dynamic. The next cluster of poems expands on a dimension of Catullan friendship that has already been touched on in poem 16: the special fusion of sexual desire and poetic creation.

Poems 35, 36 and 50: sex and text

Many of the erotic relationships that Catullus describes in the polymetrics involve three (or, in one case, four) people, even where the romance proper is two-way. As noted above, the erotic triangles of poems 11 and 15 consist of two men defining their friendship, first against a rejected woman, and then via a prized boy. When we study the male friendship bond in poems 35, 36 and 50, we find that not only is eroticism a major component, but sexuality blurs into textuality: that is, erotic passion (in both its homosexual and heterosexual varieties) and literary passion go hand in hand.

A good example of Catullus' blending of the sexual and the textual is poem 35. Playfully addressing his roll of papyrus, Catullus asks it to convey an invitation to his *sodalis* ('brother-in-arms') Caecilius, who is, we are told in the poem's first line, a 'tender poet' (the Latin word for tender, *tener*, was often used of young girls and of effeminate men, and possibly has erotic connotations here). Catullus urges Caecilius to take a holiday from his girlfriend and pay him (Catullus) a visit in Verona. Yet instead of poking fun at Caecilius' attachment to the girl, as might be expected, the poet tries a different approach. He conjures up her allurements, so sympathetically, in fact, that he could almost be said to share his friend's desire for her. Looking ahead to Caecilius' departure, Catullus pictures the 'radiant' (*candida*) girl calling after Caecilius 'a thousand times', clutching at his neck with both her hands, and 'dying of helpless love' for him. And Catullus can see why (13-18):

> Since she read his unfinished
> *Mistress of Dindymus*, from then on
> Flames have licked at the poor girl's very marrow.
> I don't blame you, girl more discerning
> Than the Muse Sappho: Caecilius' *Great*
> *Mother* is tantalisingly incomplete.

The girl's intense love for Caecilius springs from her reading of his unfinished poem *Mistress of Dindymus* (presumably a version of the myth of the Near Eastern goddess Cybele, the 'Great Mother', who came from Mount Dindymus in modern Turkey; if this poem indeed existed, it is now lost). For the girl, literary appreciation grows into erotic desire, as she extends her regard for the poem to its author. Another implied element in the poem's mingling of sex and text is the Cybele myth itself, which is sexual in character (see Chapter 5); it must have formed the subject-matter of Caecilius' poem.

Catullus' identification with the girl becomes explicit at the end of the poem, when he addresses her directly and confesses that he, too, finds the *Great Mother* charmingly (*venuste*) unfinished. Here Catullus is offering Caecilius an oblique compliment: since the new poem has inflamed the heart of a pretty and discerning girl, and enticed Catullus too, it must be a success. Actually, the compliment is twofold, for Catullus' earlier description of the girl (from *Caecilius*' perspective, significantly) suggests that the poet wouldn't mind being the one she kisses and throws her arms around. Not only is Caecilius' *poem* tantalising, Catullus intimates, so is his girl.

It's a deft compliment, to be sure – but other parts of poem 35 seem to work to counteract it. Catullus' reference in 5-6 to 'certain observations' of his regarding Caecilius' poem is couched in mock-serious language, but clearly these observations are important enough that he is anxious to convey them. Though winningly stated, Catullus' directive that Caecilius come hear his opinion is forceful. Twice he terms his friend's poem *incohata*, incomplete; we may wonder if he is trying to hammer the point home, if he wants to make Caecilius realise that the poem needs more work. It seems the *Mistress of Dindymus* has won over Catullus' heart, or rather his liver (the seat of erotic passion in ancient medical theory), but not his mind.

The erotic and the poetic are just as tightly interwoven in the next poem in the collection, so it will be useful to consider the two poems as a pair. Poem 35, we have seen, hinges on the seductive power of Caecilius' writing; Catullus is doubly seduced, by the poem and by his friend's mistress (who is herself inflamed by the *Mistress of Dindymus*). Poem 36 is a kind of flip-side to poem 35, for it presents the same situation, only inverted. Again, there is a love-affair, in which a poem by one of Catullus' contemporaries performs a key role. Now, however, the poem in question is the *Annales* by Volusius (both the text and the identity of its author are lost, but it was likely a ponderous historical epic). Catullus' verdict on the *Annales* in line 1 is harsh, and succinct: it's *cacata charta* ('shat-on sheets'), that is, toilet paper.

Such waste paper can be put to only one good use by literary lovers: it must be burned. Catullus' *puella*, the poet informs us, previously made a vow to the goddess Venus and her attendant Cupids (4-8):

> If I were brought back to her
> And if I stopped lobbing brutal iambics
> She'd offer up the worst poet's most select
> Work to the slow-footed god
> For sizzling on ill-fated firewood.

If Catullus would be reconciled with her and stop attacking her in his poems, the girl promised she would offer as a holy sacrifice 'the worst poet's most select work' – which we take to mean the *Annales*. In fact the sacrifice will not be granted to Venus herself but to her husband Vulcan, the blacksmith-god of fire. Vulcan is lame, hence Catullus' epithet 'slow-footed'; this is also a punning reference to the lumbering pace of a bad line of verse (Greek and Latin verses are made up of metrical units called 'feet', and in classical Latin the word *pes* could signify either a physical or a metrical foot). Much as ugly Vulcan is mocked and overshadowed by his beautiful wife Venus in myth, Volusius, we may infer, is outclassed by Catullus and his clever girlfriend.

Against Volusius' 'provincial dullness' (19) Catullus contrasts the girl's 'witty' (*lepide*) vow (10), which he also terms, understatedly, 'not un-charming', *neque invenustum* (17). A pun here reminds us it's no coincidence that charming (*venustus*) poetry is the domain of the goddess of love: the name *Venus* and the adjective *venustus* are etymologically connected. Perhaps the phrase 'not un-charming', then, has the secondary meaning in this context of 'not inappropriate to Venus' or 'not unworthy of Venus'. Indeed, the girl's vow as Catullus quotes it in lines 6-7 is neatly worded: *Electissima pessimi poetae/ Scripta*, with its series of *s* and *p* sounds, approximates the hissing of the poetry-scrolls on the sacred fire.

And yet the poem invites more questions. Is Catullus *himself* the worst of poets, his vicious iambics the 'most select work' to be burned? He must have stopped writing iambics about the girl, since that was the condition of the vow being fulfilled, and indeed the vow has been 'duly rendered' (15). Perhaps the old iambics are sacrificed along with – or instead of – the *Annales*. Why shouldn't Catullus, playfully or otherwise, label himself the 'worst of poets', when his beloved is the 'worst of girls' (*pessima ... puella*, 9)? This reading becomes more attractive upon noting that, in poem 49, Catullus explicitly refers to himself as *pessimus poeta* – the 'worst of poets', the same phrase (except in case-ending) that appears at 36.6.

The erotic triangle of poem 36 involves two people (Catullus and his girl) and one poem, Volusius' *Annales*. With a man and a woman forming a bond, sexually and intellectually, through their mutual rejection of bad art, 36 is unique in the Catullan corpus. But it reiterates the aesthetic-erotic program laid out in poems 2 and 3: Catullus again emphasises charm and playfulness (*iocose*, compare *iocari* at 2.6). The poet's mock-solemn prayer to Venus at the end of 36 corresponds to 3's mock-elegiac tone. And significantly, both poems begin with invocations to 'Venuses and Cupids' – these would seem to be the *puella's* personal deities.

The reappearance of the phrase *pessimus poeta* in poem 49 (a tongue-in-cheek letter of thanks to Cicero) pointedly alludes to 36.6. Catullus, in 49, may be signalling his intention to hark back to earlier motifs. For the *next* poem in the corpus, 50, deals at length and more overtly than before with the constant exchange between poetics and the erotic.

Poem 50 is a verse epistle to Catullus' friend and fellow poet Licinius (almost certainly the orator and poet C. Licinius Calvus, author of lost neoteric elegies, epigrams, and a miniature epic titled *Io*). Catullus fondly reminisces over the previous evening, which the two men spent together, dallying over Catullus' writing-tablets (4-13):

Each of us, scribbling verses,
Played around with one metre, then another,
Topping up the jokes and the wine.
And I went away on fire
From your charm, Licinius, and clever quips,
So that food held no appeal for wretched me,
Nor did sleep seal my eyes in rest,
But wild with excitement I tossed and turned
Over the bed, longing to see sunlight,
That I might be with you and talk.

Catullus describes himself as 'wretched' (*miserum*), 'on fire' (*incensus*), and gripped by a 'wild excitement' (*furore*); he says he cannot eat or sleep. Catullus' self-portrait is indebted to Homer's description of Achilles, grieving for his beloved comrade Patroclus, at *Iliad* 24.4-6. In the work of the Augustan poets who followed Catullus, these symptoms become the conventional ones of love-sickness. So Sextus Propertius (born *c.* 54-47 BC) begins the first of his *Elegies*: 'Cynthia first ensnared hapless [*miserum*] me with her darling eyes [*ocellis*]', and claims in the same poem that 'this frenzy [*furor*] has not waned for a whole year now' (1.7).

However, poem 50 also revives the ebullient playfulness of the 'sparrow poems'. Two cognates of the verb *ludere* ('to play') occur in the first five lines, and the poem is sprinkled with terms such as *iocus* (joke), *lepos* (charm) and *facetiae* (banter). The phrase *modo hoc modo illoc* – 'now in this [metre], now in that' – in line 5 instantly brings to mind poem 3's nearly identical *modo huc modo illuc* (line 9), used of the hopping sparrow. Toward the end of the poem, Catullus bestows affectionate pet-names on his friend, *iucundus*, 'charmer', and *ocellus*, 'little eye' (the same word that is used of the girl's 'swollen little eyes' at 3.18). In short, poem 50 combines the erotic play of poems 2 and 3 with the devotion to (love-)poetry that distinguishes poems 35 and 36. It further promotes the aesthetic values underpinning Catullus' work, though it does not explicitly define them.

At least one crucial question about poem 50 still remains unanswered: what ought we to make of the poem's unmistakable homoeroticism? Rather than posit male friendship as a relation distinct from (and superior to) a love relationship, as in poem 11, here Catullus suggests that friendship and romantic or sexual love are not necessarily separate realms (see

Chapter 7 for a discussion of *amicitia* and *amor*). It will be instructive to turn again to Sedgwick's *Between Men*, where we find a way of thinking about male relationships that differs considerably from the paradigm in our culture, which tends to divide heterosexual 'male bonding' very sharply from male homosexual desire (for example, male locker-room camaraderie is often accompanied by intense homophobia). For the purposes of discussing Catullan friendship I borrow the term 'homosocial desire' from Sedgwick, who defines it thus:

> 'Homosocial' is a word occasionally used in history and the social sciences, where it describes social bonds between persons of the same sex .... To draw the 'homosocial' ... into the orbit of 'desire,' of the potentially erotic, then, is to hypothesise the potential unbrokenness of a continuum between homosocial and homosexual.[4]

Sedgwick's proposition – in sum, that the social bond between male friends and the sexual bond between male lovers are not polar opposites, but are simply different points on the same continuum – certainly comes closer to Roman attitudes to sex and gender than modern Western notions.

However, such a continuum was never assumed universally or unproblematically, not even in Greece and Rome. Roman moralists censured men who displayed what was perceived as an excessive interest in sex with other men (or with women, for that matter), and sexual relationships between adult citizen men were never normalised. In poem 50, Catullus refers to himself and Licinius as *delicatus*, 'refined', a word that also had the pejorative sense of 'overly fastidious' or 'precious' (Cicero rather scornfully terms a *beau monde* dinner party *delicatus* at *Letters to*

Atticus 2.14.1). Catullus' use of this ambivalent term is risqué, prompting readers to query where on the continuum his desire for Licinius lies.

Catullan Self-Address

Poem 51: love and leisure

Taking up the dominant theme of the poems discussed in Chapter 3, poem 51, like 50, unites the poetic with the erotic. Here, sex and text are identified as the twin aspects of *otium*, leisure – a morally ambivalent commodity in Roman society, which allows Catullus and Licinius to spend their days versifying and drinking. More than the uncertain value of leisure, though, Catullus' use of the rhetorical technique of self-address is significant. Addressing himself in the poem's last stanza, he raises questions about how Catullus-the-author differs from the speaking voice that narrates the poem, and how the two interact.

The first three stanzas of poem 51 make up a relatively close translation of a love poem by Sappho, whom Catullus imitated in 11. Of the nine books of poetry Sappho is said to have written, only one complete poem and assorted fragments survive. Probably the best-known of all is the lyric usually numbered 31, in which the speaker gazes at her beloved engaged in a *tête-à-tête* with a male rival. Sappho's last two stanzas recount the intense physical symptoms of a lover's jealousy (translated here by John Addington Symonds):

Yea, my tongue is broken, and through and through me
'Neath the flesh impalpable fire runs tingling;

4. *Catullan Self-Address*

Nothing see mine eyes, and a noise of roaring
    Waves in my ears sounds;
Sweat runs down in rivers, a tremor seizes
All my limbs, and paler than grass in autumn,
Caught by pains of menacing death, I falter.

It is not surprising that this erotic triangle and the wrenching jealousy it provokes in the narrator (which Sappho captures so vividly) should have appealed to Catullus. He renders most of the poem faithfully in Latin, though deviating from the original to address his beloved by her name – Lesbia:

That man seems to me like a god,
And even (if it is right to say so) surpasses the gods,
Who, sitting across from you, again and again
    Glances and listens

To you sweetly laughing, which tears away at
All my senses: for whenever, Lesbia,
I catch sight of you, there's nothing left of
    The words in my mouth,

But my tongue thickens, under my skin
A delicate flame flickers, my ears echo with their own ringing,
My eyes are shuttered
    In double night.

Catullus' spare language, free from many of his usual 'Alexandrian' embellishments (neologisms, diminutives and the like), has a certain reverent solemnity; in the first two lines alone there are two references to divinity and one to *fas*, moral rightness. In the catalogue of love-ailments that follows (here the parallel with poem 50 is obvious), the only Alexandrian flourishes the poet allows himself are the onomatopoeic *tintinant* ('[my ears] resound/ring', 11) and a transferred epithet, *gemina* ('twin' or 'double', 11), ingeniously switched from its expected referent *lumina* ('eyes') to *nocte* ('night'). Otherwise, the diction is simple enough that it does not ironise the poet's claim to have lost his eloquence.

After line 12, however, comes an abrupt about-face. Catullus (no change of speaker is indicated) suddenly pulls back and chastises himself for overindulging in leisure (*otium*). Excessive leisure, the Romans suspected, made men debauched and effeminate; citizens were expected to limit their leisure time accordingly, even (or especially) wealthy men who had no financial incentive to do so. Cicero's famous endorsement of 'leisure with honour' (*cum dignitate otium*, *On Behalf of Sestius* 98) suggests the paradox of *otium*: though a gentleman must have time for cultural and political pursuits (which distinguishes him from a common tradesman), too much or ill-spent free time renders a man idle and therefore womanish. *Otium* is the polar opposite of business, *negotium*, even on the level of etymology (the word *negotium* is formed from *nec otium*, literally, 'not leisure').

The fourth stanza of Catullus' poem, a complete departure from Sappho's Greek, confronts the negative potential of *otium*:

> Leisure, Catullus, is bad for you:
> You revel in leisure, and get overexcited.
> Leisure has brought down kings before,
>   And flourishing cities.

These lines, so different in tone from what has gone before, give the poem a sardonic twist: the 'joke' is that, despite portraying himself as being at the mercy of his physical sensations, Catullus in fact has enough presence of mind to offer a self-appraisal. Of course, the cool appraisal belies the evident sincerity of lines 1-12. His final warning to himself in lines 15-16 – that leisure has ruined kings and great cities – seems overblown. True, leisure has provided Catullus this opportunity to neglect business affairs and instead translate a poem by Sappho, decadently assuming a woman's voice. But only for a short while; after all, the fruit of the poet's leisure is a single poem – hardly a danger to the 'flourishing cities' ruled by Rome. Nevertheless, there is a dark edge to his hyperbole. For the archetype of the great city laid low is Troy, its downfall precipitated by the desire of one man (the Trojan prince Paris) for a beautiful woman (Helen) who belonged to another man (the Greek king Menelaus). Illicit love is manifestly the province of *otium*.

During the nineteenth and early twentieth centuries, the critical response to the final stanza of Catullus 51 was unenthusiastic, to say the least. Most critics declared that it ruined what was otherwise a fine translation of Sappho; it was generally thought to be either spurious, or a separate lyric fragment that had been mistakenly affixed to the 'real' ending at line 12.

Now, however, Catullus' fourth stanza is generally accepted as the poem's proper conclusion.[1] Indeed, it can easily be read as an example of the self-awareness that is so typical of Catullus the author. As we know, Catullus does not have reservations about depicting himself in an unflattering light (though he reacts angrily when *others* do so); that is, he often portrays himself as powerless, unmanned and unloved. Nor is he averse to stepping outside himself, as it were, to comment on his own actions. With the final stanza of poem 51, the poet lets drop the narrative thread on which the reader's empathy hangs – his tale of suffering in love – and abruptly shifts into the mode of meta-narrative. The 'I' who has narrated the poem thus far is silenced, by another 'I' – 'another' first-person narrator, or distinct internal voice, who responds to the previous narrator, addressing him in the second person (as 'Catullus').

That the competing voices are not ultimately reconciled or balanced may seem odd to today's readers, who tend to privilege a poem's 'resolution' above all else. Yet in the case of Catullus, it is the accumulation of unresolved contrasts, such as we find in 51, that in large part makes his body of work compelling (for what real-life lover ever could resolve his or her conflicting emotions?).

Poem 8: seductive rhetoric

Likewise, there is no tidy resolution in the most important example of Catullan self-address, poem 8. Constructed around antitheses, the poem is a kind of rhetorical juggling-act, in which the narrator(s) entertain different, sometimes conflicting, impulses. In the poem, Catullus tries to conquer his passion for his estranged *puella* by telling himself that his good times with her are over, that he should not pursue her when she avoids him. As the poet weighs his wretched present against a happier past, and anxiously looks to the future, we see his ego splinter into the second and third persons:

> Pathetic Catullus, stop acting like a fool
> And what you know you've lost, admit you've lost it.
> Once the days shone bright for you,
> When you kept on going wherever your girl led,
> A girl we loved as no other will ever be loved.
> There, when we got up to so much fun,
> Which you wanted – and she didn't *not* want,
> Yes, the days shone bright for you.
> Now, though, she doesn't want you, so, you pushover, don't you

Chase after someone who runs away, or mope,
But with a stubborn resolve chin up, be firm.
Farewell, girl. Now Catullus is firm,
He doesn't look for you or ask after you, reluctant girl.
But you'll be sorry when you're not asked after.
You wretch – what kind of life is in store for you?
Who'll chase you now? In whose eyes will you seem pretty?
Whom will you love, now? You'll be described as – whose girl?
Whom will you kiss? Whose lips will you bite?
But you, Catullus, you're determined – be firm.

To begin, the poet addresses 'Catullus' in the second person (hence, 'what *you* know you've lost'), driving a wedge between himself and this *Miser Catulle* – yet we know that the poet (or rather, the voice that narrates the poem) *also is Catullus*. Next, this same voice – the poem's *ego*, its 'I' – lingers over 'Catullus''s (the other's) happy memories of his love-affair. The *ego*'s close identification with 'Catullus' in lines 5-6, where the first-person plural is used ('A girl *we* loved ...'), signals that the two Catulluses are in fact dual aspects of the same subjectivity. And the distinction between them is unstable – we cannot easily tell where one blurs into the other.

At line 9 *ego* abandons the past and turns back to the present, once again enjoining 'Catullus' (now berated as a 'pushover') to stand firm. By bidding the girl goodbye at line 12, he would seem to resolve his dilemma, but he does not. The third-person statement 'Now Catullus is firm' is simply not as convincing as the first-person ('I am firm'); while the latter implies (literal) single-mindedness, the former suggests a disintegration of the self, of self-purpose.

Then, at line 15, *ego* directs a series of rhetorical questions to the absent girl: whom will you love? Whom will you kiss? As the questions become vividly specific (whose lips will you bite?), we sense that the narrator is reliving a moment in the past when the girl nibbled *his* lips ... though in the very next, and final, verse, he springs forward again to the present, desperately reminding 'Catullus' to 'be firm' (19).

The see-saw quality of poem 8 is frequently mentioned by commentators. As the poem's argument swings between two opposing (internalised) perspectives – we might call them 'I-in-the-present' and 'Catullus-in-the-past' – so Catullus' language doubles back on itself. Numerous repetitions strike the eye, including *obdura*, 'be firm', which appears at the ends of lines 11 and 19, and its cognate *obdurat* ('[Catullus] is firm') at the end of line 12; the phrase *at tu* ('But you ...') is used to begin lines 14 and 19; line 8 is a repetition of line 3, exact but for one word, *vere* ('yes' or 'truly'), which replaces the earlier *quondam* ('once').

In addition to these examples we perceive more vague echo-effects such as *amata* and *amabitur* (literally, 'she was loved' and 'she will be loved') in line 5; *nec rogabit*, 'he will not ask', in 13 and *rogaberis nulla*, 'you won't be asked for', in 14; and even some half-rhymes, for instance, *nulla*, *vita* and *bella*, capping off lines 14, 15 and 16 respectively. Constant repetition often makes poem 8 feel like a dialogue between two voices. On stage or screen, it might run something like this:

> *Catullus1*: Pathetic Catullus, you know you've lost the good thing you had with that girl.
> *Catullus2*: (reminiscing) Once the days were bright for you, when you followed her around; we loved that girl –
> *Catullus1*: – as no other girl's ever been loved.
> *Catullus2*: We had so much fun. Oh, you wanted it –
> *Catullus1*: – and she didn't *not* want it!
> *Catullus2*: Yes, the days were bright then, they really were ...

Catullus1: But *now*, she doesn't want it. So you can't want it either anymore, you weakling!

Yet despite this dialogic pattern, it's never easy to disentangle one perspective from the other, to separate 'I-in-the-present' from 'Catullus-in-the-past'. Their interconnectedness is a measure of Catullus' skill, because perhaps the most extraordinary thing about poem 8, though it is sometimes overlooked, is that the 'two voices' of the poem are, in formal terms, only one. Poem 8's duality is an effect of extremely subtle rhetoric: no formal elements of the poem indicate that different voices articulate the perspectives of 'I-in-the-present' and 'Catullus-in-the-past'. I submit that a single voice, however inconsistent it may be, expresses – *ventriloquises* is the better word – both the narration of the present-tense *ego* and those sentiments we might instinctively attribute to the individual 'voice' of 'Catullus-in-the-past'.

Poem 8 is one of the most difficult texts in the corpus, with few critics agreeing on how to read it. One Catullus scholar, Ellen Greene, gives an interpretation at variance with the one just offered above. On Greene's view, the narrative self breaks apart completely, into two distinct voices. The 'speaker', Greene argues, tries to dissuade the 'lover' (or, to use my phrase, 'Catullus-in-the-past') from his hopeless passion, while the 'lover' indulges in idealised memories of the past. At line 9, says Greene,

> When the speaker breaks away from his imaginative vision of past happiness and calls 'Catullus' '*impotens,*' it is also an expression of his own 'impotence' in being unable to persuade 'Catullus' to stop desiring the *puella*. We can hear desperation and urgency in the word *impotens* in that it ... links speaker and lover in their mutual failure.[2]

71

Indeed, this explanation is cogent. But it seems to imply that rhetoric breaks down in poem 8; because the two voices of 'speaker' and 'lover' cannot be reconciled, the result is a 'mutual failure' of speech. I prefer to read poem 8 as an ironic – and therefore typically Catullan – demonstration of just how easily an effective speaker may be persuaded by *his own* rhetoric. The Catullus who tells himself he must give up a damaging love is the same Catullus who assiduously recounts the particulars of his life with the girl. That this exercise is in some way pleasurable (though the pleasure is mixed with jealousy and grief) we should not doubt, for the poet keeps reverting to it.

Do the narrator's memories of the affair flood back unheeded, we may wonder, or does the poet bear rather more responsibility for his predicament, by consciously dredging these memories up? It is not the happy past itself, but the *act* of recalling and succumbing to it that enthralls Catullus. In other words, he seduces himself with speech, a spellbound audience to his own linguistic performance. The French theorist Roland Barthes captures this phenomenon in a passage from his meditation on love and language, *A Lover's Discourse*:

> I take a role: I am *the one who is going to cry*; and I play this role for myself, and *it makes me cry*: I am my own theater. And seeing me cry this way makes me cry all the more; and if the tears tend to decrease, I quickly repeat to myself the lacerating phrase that will set them flowing again.[3]

Barthes' assertion that 'I am my own theater' brings us to another aspect of poem 8 (and Catullan self-address in general): its performative quality. For there is something obviously stagey about this poem. 'The Jealous Man is on stage, and we come in on his monologue', critic Paul Veyne comments of it. Veyne reminds us not to be fooled by what looks like sincerity on the poet's part, for it is only a performance (albeit a magnificent one). Poem 8 'is spoken as it is being lived .... A masterpiece thus set forth can pass for a cry from the heart.'[4]

Elsewhere in the same volume, Veyne compares the self-revelation of a Catullus or Propertius to the confessional pose of a modern-day pop singer. The parallel is, I think, extremely apt: when either a pop singer or a Roman elegist sings a love song, he likely isn't singing about himself – and what's more, in the case of the pop singer, we *know* he (or she) probably isn't. When Marvin Gaye's classic song 'I Heard It Through the Grapevine' plays on the radio, very few listeners would take its first-person lyrics at face value and assume that Gaye sings to his real-life lover. Instead of 'speaking from the heart', what Gaye did, and other pop singers do, more often is to *mime* the speech of lovers. And wouldn't the same hold true for Catullus? He mimes the speech of his stage persona, a lover, also called 'Catullus'.

Poem 8 remind us of the difficulties of distinguishing the *ego* from the poet; truth from fiction; subtle rhetoric for artless confession. As Veyne rightly concludes, 'It is Catullus' *art* that is sincere.'[5]

Crossing the Threshold

Poems 61 and 62: the epithalamia

Poem 61 initiates a series of nine poems quite distinct from the fifty-six polymetrics that came before.[1] Whereas the earlier poems tend to be fairly short – generally twenty lines or shorter – these are much lengthier, ranging from 24 lines (poem 65) to a substantial 160 (68B) and even up to 408 (poem 64). The poet's concerns in this section are different, too, as is the cast of his rhetoric. Absent are the bitter personal disputes and light-hearted camaraderies that formed the subject-matter of so many of the polymetrics; in place of occasional poetry, this series offers ambitious narratives and (generically speaking) higher themes borrowed from myth and ritual. (There are a few exceptions to this rule, however: the polymetric 34 is a reverent choral hymn to Diana, while 67 is a whimsical dialogue between a man and a door.)

Beginning the series is a pair of epithalamia or wedding poems (the singular *epithalamium* is a Latinised Greek word, and means 'by the bedchamber'). The first, composed in a graceful, spare lyric metre, celebrates what was evidently a historical marriage between the nobleman Manlius Torquatus and a woman named Iunia Aurunculeia. Since weddings in the Roman world were public occasions, Catullus dons the mantle of a public poet to narrate poem 61. This persona could hardly differ more from the fractured *ego* of poem 8, the Catullus who interrogates and responds to himself as if he were trapped in a hall of mirrors. Rather, Catullus' voice in 61 is authoritative, and speaks of matters outside the poet's self.

Moreover, Catullus' role in 61 is twofold. As well as being the poem's narrator, he is also a kind of master of ceremonies, summoning the marriage-god Hymen, instructing a chorus of young girls to sing wedding-hymns, and, later, dispensing stern advice to the newlywed couple. Indeed, the poet-speaker's attempt to control participants in the wedding may have had a political dimension. In a chaotic society like that of Roman Italy during the first century BC, the authority asserted here by Catullus – who speaks on behalf of a whole community – possibly responded to people's concerns that the social order was under threat.[2]

Poem 61 opens with an extended prayer to Hymen, the Greco-Roman deity of marriage. In the course of summoning Hymen to the nuptials, Catullus frequently alludes to elements of the Roman marriage ritual. Some of these require explanation. In the second stanza of 61, for example, the poet asks Hymen to come to the ceremony wearing a wreath of marjoram, a flame-coloured veil and yellow shoes. These were the traditional accoutrements of Hymen and, by extension, the Roman bride herself: the so-called Aldobrandini frieze, a late first-century BC wall-painting of a wedding scene that is now in the Vatican Museum, depicts a bride dressing in the traditional white tunic and orange veil. Although the symbolic value of each item is not perfectly clear, it is likely that the *flammeum* (veil) was thought to represent the bride's bloodshed at her first sexual encounter. Marjoram, which produces reddish flowers, fits into the same broad colour-scheme, as does the prescribed saffron colour of the bride's shoes. Catullus makes reference in poem 61 both to Iunia's 'golden little feet' (160) and to her *flammeum* (115).

Next, Catullus commands Hymen to join in the wedding songs and shake his pine-wood torch (*pinea taeda*): such torches were a standard feature of Roman weddings, lighting the route of the wedding procession from the bride's home to the groom's home (called the *deductio*, this, perhaps the most important part of the ceremony, dramatises the bride's passage from one household, and one stage of her life, to another). The poem's colour-imagery is enhanced by Catullus' description of the torch-flames as 'golden tresses' (95).

As stated above, ancient weddings of aristocrats often were public, communal events. Unlike wedding ceremonies in Western countries today, which are usually planned according to the tastes of the bride and groom, Roman rites were dictated by tradition, and matches were typically arranged by two families wishing to cement their alliance. Roman brides and grooms were often very young by modern standards – girls were expected to marry before their fifteenth birthday, and young men before the age of twenty-five at the latest.[3] We have no way of knowing the exact ages of Catullus' Iunia and Manlius.

In four consecutive stanzas starting at line 56, the scope of Catullus' narrative widens steadily, from the realm of the specific and domestic – 'Into the hands of an unruly youth/ You give over a blooming young girl/ From the embrace of/ Her mother', is how the poet invokes Hymen (56-9) – to the entire state (*res publica*). Without Hymen's aid, the poet continues, Venus can do nothing that is in keeping with 'good reputation' (*fama ... bona*, 62), an all-important quality within the small, close-knit world of the Roman upper class. Catullus goes on (66-75):

Without you [Hymen] no house can
Produce heirs, and no parent
Can rely on his offspring – but he can,

With your goodwill. Who would dare
Compare with this god?

The land that lacks your rites
Cannot put forth protectors
Of its borders – but it can,
With your goodwill. Who would dare
Compare with this god?

Focussing initially on one family home (*domus*), Catullus then expands his view to encompass the Roman state as a whole. The relation between *domus* and *res publica* was extremely close: the Romans did not perceive a significant divide between private and public life, but tended to view the *domus* as a microcosm of greater Roman values. In Catullus' wedding poem, as in his Rome, a good personal reputation, the begetting of heirs to continue one's family line, and, society-wide, the creation of a generation of 'protectors' of Rome's borders, are all crucial and interdependent.

At line 75 the poet's long invocation to Hymen ends, and in the next stanza the bridal *deductio* commences. Or at least, Catullus tries to get it started, but the bride is reluctant. (In most epithalamia, not just those in Latin, the bride is characterised as modest and timid.) 'Undo the door-bolts', he orders (addressing slaves, presumably); he entreats the weeping Aurunculeia to come out of her house, and reassures her that her husband-to-be is 'not light' (97) and is not involved with an 'awful adulteress' (98).

His words may seem strange to readers who are not familiar with the genre. Why does Catullus refer so openly to the bride's anxieties? At modern weddings, any reference to infidelity is studiously avoided. However, acknowledging the dangers associated with marriage is an epithalamic convention. Typically the poet cites these dangers in a negative construction, in order to exclude them, ultimately, from the harmonious world of the poem. The most famous wedding poem in the English language, Edmund Spenser's 'Epithalamion' (1595), incorporates a lengthy catalogue of potential threats to marital concord. Its delicately mocking tone simultaneously invokes and defuses dangerous forces (334-7; 343-4):

> Let no lamenting cryes, nor dolefull teares,
> Be heard all night within nor yet without.
> Ne let false whispers, breeding hidden feares,
> Breake gentle sleepe with misconceived dout ...
> Ne let hob Goblins, names whose sence we see not,
> Fray us with things that be not.

Catullus, instead of providing such a catalogue, scatters allusions to the dangers of marriage throughout the text of 61.

In this passage from 'Epithalamion', Spenser does not imitate Catullus specifically, but conforms to the wider tradition of epithalamic writing. Yet other English poets have selected Catullus' epithalamium in particular as a model for their own efforts. One simile from 61, which appears twice in the poem with slight variations, has proved uniquely appealing. Addressing the bride, Catullus likens her love for Manlius to a vine and trees in a forest (102-5):

> But just as the pliant vine
> Winds itself around nearby trees,
> He will be tangled up in your
> Embrace.

Earlier, in his invocation to Hymen, the poet beseeched the god to summon Iunia to her new home (33-5),

Twining her mind with love
As grasping ivy, reaching this way and that,
Enfolds the tree.

The 'vine and tree' comparison enjoyed great popularity in Britain through the late sixteenth and seventeenth centuries, possibly because English writers preferred to imitate memorable passages of Catullus, not whole poems. Sir Philip Sidney was one of the first to reuse the image in the Third Eclogues of his 1593 *Arcadia* (the 'Old Arcadia'), where the speaker Dicus beseeches the sun to grace the nuptials of 'The honest bridegroom and the bashful bride' (15-18),

Whose loves may ever bide,
Like to the elm and vine,
With mutual embracements them to twine;
In which delightful pain,
O Hymen long their coupled joys maintain.

Shakespeare's contemporary Ben Jonson adapted the same image in a wedding song included in his classicising court masque of 1606, *Hymenaei*. 'Let ivy not so bind/ As when your arms are twined', Jonson urges the newlyweds. However, Jonson and other poets of his generation took as their chief source for the vine and tree not poem 61, but poem 62, in which the conceit is greatly expanded.

Like 61, 62 is a choral wedding poem, but it takes the distinct form of a competition between two choirs, one composed of girls and the other of young men. The wedding it celebrates is not specified, and in all likelihood was imaginary. In alternating stanzas, the male choir sings in favour of marriage for women, the female choir against. When the latter declares that a girl who is no longer a virgin 'loses her pure bloom' (46), and is 'neither pleasing to boys nor held dear by girls' (47),[4] the young men counter thus (49-58):

> As the unwed vine that grows on bare earth
> Never lifts herself up, never produces the ripe grape,
> But bowing her delicate body with stooping weight
> Now even touches her topmost shoot to her stem;
> No farmers, no oxen have looked after her:
> But if this vine by chance is married to a husband elm,
> Many farmers, many oxen have looked after her:
> Just so a girl, while she remains untouched, grows old neglected;
> When she has made an equal marriage at the right time,
> She is more precious to her husband, and less bothersome to
>   her parents.

What this passage implies about Roman attitudes to gender roles is striking. An unmarried woman is presented as defective, so abnormally delicate (*tenera*) that she cannot even support the burden of her own body. Men ignore her; her parents are annoyed by her. The 'equal' (*par*) marriage the young men advocate is, by modern standards, nothing of the sort – whereas the vine is completely dependent on its host elm, the elm relies on the vine for adornment only. That a Roman woman's paramount duty was to marry and bear children is made even clearer at the end of the poem, with a starkly legalistic formulation: 'Your virginity is not all yours', the men's chorus tells the bride (62). 'One-third is your father's, one-third is granted your mother, / Only a third belongs to you' (63-4).

Returning now to the *deductio* of 61, when Catullus finally sees the bride emerge from her house, he turns to the boys in the wedding party and bids them to start singing. But the song is no longer *io Hymen Hymenaee*, which has been poem 61's refrain thus far. Instead, the poet now calls for 'impudent Fescennine banter' (*Fescennina iocatio*, 120). This ribald verse-mockery, named after the Etruscan town Fescennia (which presumably excelled in it), was common at Roman weddings and military triumphs. Like the poet's earlier reference to the bride's anxieties, his inclusion of bawdy, abusive songs indicates tolerance on the part of the Romans for potentially disruptive speech regarding marriage.

Catullus takes aim first at a *concubinus* (boy concubine) in the groom's household, who, he implies, was once the master's sexual favourite (there is an allusion to his 'love of Master forsaken' at lines 122-3). The concubine is repeatedly enjoined to 'give nuts' (124, 128, 133) to the small boys in the retinue, who would have used them as pieces in their games (walnuts were commonly scattered during wedding processions). In a broad sense the nuts connoted fertility, so they were appropriate for the occasion; but they were also regarded as tokens of childhood. By distributing nuts to the younger boys, the concubine indicates that he has now left his own childhood behind. Moreover, at lines 131-2 he is ritually shaved – for the first time, presumably. This practice also seems to have been a normal part of the Roman celebration.[5]

Catullus' Fescinnine teasing would have made the concubine – and the groom who was so fond of him – blush. But that was not its sole function. The poet-speaker's jests all point to the same concept: timeliness, the importance of engaging in behaviour that is sanctioned as appropriate for one's stage of life. This is what the concubine is prodded to do, and later, so is the groom himself, told he must give up certain pleasures he enjoyed as a bachelor because, as a husband, 'these same [pleasures] aren't allowed' (141). For both the concubine and the groom, the transition to a new phase in life is bumpy. The groom is rumoured not to be able to keep away from slave-boys (134-6); his concubine is reluctant to scatter nuts (evidently wanting to keep them for himself) and despite his physical maturation is disdainful of women (lines 129-32). The emotional difficulty of embarking on a new stage in life – and especially the fear that this new situation will be unhappy – threaten to subvert a new marriage. Catullus acknowledges the danger, yet he defuses it with, in the groom's case, an appeal to societal norms (a married man who was overly fond of young boys was morally suspect), and in the bride's case, an appeal to her power to prevent infidelity ('... beware of denying your husband what he asks for,/ Lest he go somewhere else to ask', 144-6).

At line 159, the bride finally enters her new home, the *domus* of her husband's family. The moment of her stepping over the threshold would have been tense, since to stumble was considered a bad omen (hence the still-observed custom for grooms to carry their brides through the doorway on the wedding night). We now perceive that the narrative of poem 61 has followed the wedding party's route across town: it begins at the bride's house, with the poet-speaker entreating the girl to come out; it then moves through the streets as the Fescennine verses are chanted; lastly it reaches the groom's house.

The following several stanzas chart the bride's progress through the interior of the house and into the bedchamber. Yet the bride herself remains passive as she comes closer to her new husband, and to adulthood. 'Let go of the little girl's little arm', Catullus commands a boy-page (174-5); 'settle the little girl [on the bed]', he orders the attendant matrons (181). Representations like this of the bride as a passive object – an object that is moved around by other people throughout the wedding – became commonplace in English epithalamia of the sixteenth and seventeenth centuries. In the 'Epithalamion' (which was a more decisive influence on later English wedding poetry than even Catullus 61), Spenser takes on not only the prescribed roles of poet-speaker and master of ceremonies, but a third – that of husband, for the wedding he writes of was his own. (He married Elizabeth Boyle in Ireland in 1594.) When the time for the consummation of the marriage draws near, Spenser addresses his bride's attendants (298-304):

> Now day is doen, and night is nighing fast:
> Now bring the Bryde into the brydall boures.
> Now night is come, now soone her disarray,
> And in her bed her lay;
> Lay her in lillies and in violets,
> And silken courteins over her display,
> And odourd sheetes, and Arras coverlets.

In her instructive book on English wedding poetry, *A Happier Eden*, Heather Dubrow offers multiple reasons why the brides in epithalamia are often depicted as passive. First, 'Such images', she observes, 'negate the fears of sexual promiscuity or even sexual energy that the marriage intensified.' The sexual 'awakening' of the bride at her marriage carried the risk that she would become vulnerable to the interest of other men and would commit adultery, thereby disgracing the rest of the family. In the case of Catullus' poem 61, the diminutives Catullus uses of the bride – such as *bracchiolus*, '[her] little arm' (174); *puellula*, 'little girl' (175, 181); *floridulus*, 'like a little flower' (186) – ironically infantilise the bride, and thus may help to play down her sexual agency. At the same time, diminutives in Catullus' verse are also associated with sexual *desirability*, as in poems 2 and 3.

Images of the bride's passivity betoken not just sexual, but overall compliance: '[These] poets both foreshadow and recommend a similar obedience after marriage', Dubrow writes. Yet Dubrow admits of another reading , one that has more positive ramifications for the epithalamic bride. 'In emphasizing that the bride is led, poets imply that she belongs to the community leading her ... they honor the bride in the very process of disempowering her', she concludes.[6]

In poem 61, as in so many wedding poems, the consummation long anticipated by the poet passes almost without remark. Catullus dedicates a single stanza to the couple's 'many thousands of love-games' (203), before expressing succinctly the hope of all the wedding party, what is (after all) the main objective of the marriage: *ludite et lubet, et brevi/ liberos dare*, 'play as you wish and soon/ produce children' (204-5). With *ludite*, Catullus again draws on the sexual suggestiveness of *ludere*, a verb of great power in the polymetrics. But the couple's sexual relationship is then directly transferred to its end-product, the 'tiny Torquatus' (209) who Catullus imagines sitting in his mother's lap and smiling up at his father.

The emphasis in the poem's concluding stanzas is on the chastity of the young would-be mother. 'May he look like his father/ Manlius' (214), Catullus wishes of the couple's future son – not so much complimenting the groom on his good looks as stressing that the children of the union must be legitimate, or dishonour will taint the family. Catullus ends on an admonitory note:

> Shut the doors, girls.
> We've played enough. But you, good
> Married couple, live well, and
> In its perpetual duty
> Train your thriving youth.

Even as he leaves the couple to begin their aforementioned love-games, he issues a veiled warning: the newlyweds must 'train' (or 'exercise' – the Latin verb has military overtones) their sexual urges so as to obey their duty as Romans. An apt pun reinforces the point. Catullus' word for duty (*munus*) can convey a sexual meaning – i.e., a person's duty to give sexual pleasure to his or her partner. Still, the seriousness of the command shouldn't be overstated, for Catullus' witty expression suggests a different, and lighter, meaning: 'Enjoy yourselves in bed' is the basic message.[7]

For most of the twentieth century, poem 61 was regarded as a sentimental portrait of a blushing bride and her groom, a joyous paean to married love. One critic at the turn of the last century praised the epithalamium's 'charm of perfect simplicity';[8] another, as recently as the 1990s, went so far as to call it 'an emotionally uncomplicated celebration of marriage as a state of utter bliss'.[9] It is my opinion that poem 61 has been consistently devalued, and that most modern writing on it has obscured the poem's ambivalence, its complex negotiations with the risks of marriage. Yet scholars are now reassessing the poem using the tools of contemporary criticism, and in particular, new approaches to the study of history and gender. Already profiting from such attention is poem 63, whose radically dissimilar (but equally sustained) engagement with the concept of transition makes it poem 61's unlikely companion-piece.

Poem 63: Attis

Perhaps the only aspect of poem 63 that is not subject to debate is its uniqueness – of that there can be no doubt. The poem is the only surviving example (apart from some scrappy fragments) in Latin or Greek of the galliambic metre, a long, rushing verse line associated with the worship of the goddess Cybele from Asia Minor. Moreover, poem 63's narrative – about a Greek adolescent named Attis who castrates himself in a frenzy of devotion to Cybele, only to repent his act – has no clear parallel in classical literature.

In all other respects, the poem is disputed. Is it semi-auto-biographical, or an impersonal display of technical virtuosity? Does Catullus glamorise Attis' actions or is the young (wo)man depicted rather as a figure to be pitied – or to be loathed? These and other ambiguities arise from Catullus' frequent juxtapositions of polar opposites: civilisation versus barbarity (and, correspondingly, Greece versus the East); male versus female; power versus servility; reason versus madness.

The poem begins *in medias res*. Attis has travelled to Phrygia (modern-day Turkey) by boat and, stepping ashore, he hastens toward the wooded grove said to be Cybele's home. Then, goaded by what Catullus calls a 'frantic madness' (4), he takes up a sharp piece of flint and 'pulls off the weights of his groin' (5). Spotting the ground with drops of blood, *she* then seizes a tambourine in her 'snow-white hands' (*niveis … manibus*, 8). The feminine adjective used here, *citata* (used with adverbial force as '[she] quickly'), signals that nothing short of a sex-change has occurred – Attis is now effectively female. She is feminised by the vivid colour-contrast in lines 7-8; white hands are conventionally a desirable attribute in women (as attested by Homer), and the blood issuing from her groin recalls a rite of passage that is quintessentially female – a bride's sexual initiation on her wedding night. What Catullus portrays here, then, is an ironic inversion of female sexual awakening.

Singing and beating on her tambourine, Attis urges her fellow devotees to follow her to the goddess's inmost forest domain. Her song exemplifies wildness, the uncivilised. She addresses her companions as 'straying cattle' (13), a telling metaphor; endowed with no more rationality than beasts, they roam the woods of Phrygia aimlessly. Attis also compares them to 'exiles heading for foreign places' (14). Indeed, as self-made exiles, they have abandoned their homes and, crucially, the societal norms that once regulated their lives. Now they follow, not a general or a philosopher, but a maddened eunuch who will lead them only deeper into the woods, and further away from civilisation.

These lines present an interesting contrast as well to an important myth of origins in Roman culture: the founding of what was to become Rome by the Trojan hero Aeneas. Like Attis, Aeneas led his exiled countrymen across the seas, but his goal was to establish a new nation, to *promote* civilisation. It may be relevant that Attis and her companions castrate themselves 'in [their] exceeding hatred of Venus' (17), for Venus in myth is Aeneas' mother. In short, Attis and her companions renounce the generative principle – and the Roman duty to raise free-born children – that Venus, the goddess of love, embodies.

In verses 21-30, Catullus describes in detail the music and dancing that accompany the worship of Cybele. Also known as the *Magna Mater* (Great Mother), Cybele was a deity of Asia Minor whose cult first arrived in Rome in 205 BC. Although primarily a goddess of fertility, she also had dominion over the wild natural world (especially mountains) and was thought to protect her followers in times of war. In ancient art, she is usually depicted wearing a turreted crown (symbolising her defensive powers), carrying a libation-bowl and/or a drum, and attended by lions (representing untamed nature). Music-making and dancing were important parts of her cult, and devotees were said to go into ecstatic raptures.[10] Cybele's cult enjoyed official recognition in Republican Rome, but its priest-hood – whose members, called *Galli*, were eunuchs – remained off-limits to Roman citizens, receiving only men of Phrygian origin. The 'uncivilised' cast of the cult, in which eunuchs played such a prominent part, meant that it was not fully assimilated to Roman state religion until the early years of the Empire, when the emperor Claudius lifted the restrictions on the goddess' worship.

In Catullus' poem, Attis leads a singing, dancing, ululating, pipe-playing, cymbal-clashing procession ever deeper into the woods, 'just like a restless heifer evading the heavy yoke' (33). The final ecstasy she has been yearning for soon dissipates, however. After too much exertion 'without Ceres' (= without food; the goddess Ceres presided over crops), the acolytes finally reach Cybele's sanctum, only to fall asleep. When Attis wakes up the following morning, 'free from whirling rage' (44), she realises 'with a clear mind' (46) what has happened – and what *she* now lacks. Alone, she returns to the shore, revis-iting the scene of her self-unmanning. The sudden disappearance of her companions is not accounted for, but whatever its cause, it serves to emphasise the fact that the devotees were not a cohesive social group akin to a family or nation; their only binding tie was their mutual (though selfish and irrational) adoration of Cybele.

Ancient poetry affords numerous examples of women in distress who deliver impassioned soliloquies from the seashore. One of these women is Catullus 64's Ariadne, abandoned by Theseus on the island of Naxos (her soliloquy will be discussed in the next chapter).[11] That Attis should conform to this type is another mark of her feminisation. Scanning the horizon, she addresses, not a man who cruelly abandoned her, but the country which she fled of her own volition (50-5):

5. Crossing the Threshold

O land that created me, land that raised me,
Whom I, unlucky, deserted, as runaway slaves
Their masters; to the groves of Ida I directed my pace,
That I might be close to snow and the frozen dens of beasts,
And, raving, come upon their hiding-places –
O where, homeland, or in what corner, do I think you lie?

The generative powers of Attis' home country – which the epithets *creatrix* ('begetter') and *genetrix* ('mother') stress – form an implicit contrast to Attis' new sterility. Equally, it is intriguing that she should compare her flight to that of a runaway slave. She, too, escaped the strictures of society in pursuit of personal freedom – but at what cost? Ironically, by divesting herself of her manhood and her rationality (two qualities that were closely connected in ancient thought), she has entered into a servitude of a different kind. In thrall to Cybele/Mother Nature, she has bound herself to all that is wild, irrational and feminine. And this time, escape is not an option: as line 55 suggests, home is irrevocably lost to her now.

At line 59, Attis begins to recall the particulars of her earlier, civilised (and, of course, male) life. Her catalogue progressively narrows from the large and impersonal to the small and intimate: 'Will I be absent from my country, property, friends, and parents?' In the next verse she conjures up the physical environment of this lost world, with its monuments of civilisation, 'the forum, the *palaestra* [ball-game area], the stadium and gymnasia' (60). Marilyn Skinner, in an important article on poem 63, describes these edifices as constituting the realm of 'male civic virtue', with their ordered social and physical activities (in the ancient world, as in the modern world, sport had non-physical dimensions as a character-building civic engagement).[12] This is the realm that Attis has excluded himself from forever.

Yet it is also a realm in which Attis, before the onset of his madness, thrived. In the pathetic core of her lament, Attis recalls her former prestige, and contrasts it to her new status as an outcast and slave-girl (62-73):

For what shape have I not assumed?
I have been a woman, I a young man, I an ephebe, I a boy;
I've been the flower of the gymnasium; I was the glory of the
    athlete's oil.
My doors were crowded, my porch was warm,
My house was draped with fresh garlands
When at sunrise I would leave my bed.
I now, shall I be called an attendant of the gods, and Cybele's
    slave-girl?
Shall I be a Maenad, I a part of myself, I a sterile man?
Shall I inhabit the cold corners of green Ida, shrouded in snow?
Shall I spend my life beneath the high peaks of Phrygia,
Where the woodland-dwelling deer, where the forest-wandering
    boar are?
Now, now I bewail what I've done – now, now I regret it.

These verses, rather than inviting our sympathy, may impose an ironicising distance between us and the speaker. When Attis asks, 'What shape have I not assumed?' she hints at a belated self-awareness. In this she resembles, at first glance, another figure from Greco-Roman myth who gains wisdom by undergoing sex change – the blind seer Tiresias, who, according to Ovid, lived for seven years as a woman. But Attis' soliloquy is undercut with irony, for it soon becomes clear that she is not any wiser for her experience. She does not mourn for her loss of family, friends or civic identity, only for her status as an object of desire; nor can she conceive of being female as anything beyond 'not-maleness', that is, the blank negation of what it is to be a man.

'I was the flower of the gymnasium', Attis recalls, lingering on the memory of her former sexual desirability. In Latin and Greek poetry, young women are often compared to flowers,[13] as at Catullus 61.87-9 and 186-8, where the word *flos* ('flower') and its cognates are used of virgin brides. Was Attis, then, feminised even *before* his self-castration? It seems clear that, at the least, the *adolescens* Attis was reluctant to take on the active (sexual) role required of adult males. Instead, he wanted always to remain a passive object of adoration. 'Through his self-mutilation', Skinner writes, '... [Attis] attempts to remain fixed at the [sexually] passive stage, in defiance of biological impulses to growth and development.' Skinner finds support for this interpretation in Greek sources, which 'regularly depict male adolescence as a liminal stage characterised by sexual ambiguity and portray the passage from youth to adulthood ... as fraught with potential for psychological misadventure, especially for those who were once renowned beauties'.[14] An additional example from mythology comes to mind: Narcissus, who spurns would-be lovers but pines for his own reflection in a pool, until he dies of self-love.

Attis goes on to juxtapose these past triumphs with her present circumstances. Once so handsome, she is now deformed, only 'part of myself' (69) – Catullus' pun renders her incomplete, ironically, by virtue of her missing (and sex-defining) 'part'. Once a free male at home in the gymnasium, she is now a servile female, 'Cybele's slave-girl' (68), haunting the wilderness. Whereas *his* porch was warm with a throng of admirers, *her* forest home is 'shrouded in snow' (70) and lonely, save for a few lurking beasts. If these juxtapositions are fairly blatant, so too is Attis' thumpingly repetitive language. In the passage quoted above, the word *ego* ('I') appears a total of thirteen times; *mihi* ('[to] me') appears in four places. The speaker's unrelenting emphasis on herself is more likely to alienate readers than rouse their sympathy.

Offended by Attis' wish to return home, Cybele orders one of her lions to drive Attis from the shore back into the woods, and back into a state of madness. When the lion approaches her, 'tender' Attis is standing beside the 'marbles of the deep', *marmora pelagi*; this metaphor emphasises Attis' delicacy, the aspect of her that is still civilised. But when the lion charges, the marbled sea gives way to 'wild thickets' (89), and *tener* becomes *demens*, 'crazed'. Catullus tells us that Attis lived out the rest of her days as Cybele's slave, and he concludes the poem with a prayer (91-3):

> Goddess, Great Goddess, Cybebe, Goddess Mistress of
>   Dindymus,
> Far from my home may all your madness lie, Lady.
> Make others ecstatic, make others raving mad.

Poem 63 is somewhat baffling to the modern reader, because one's expectations are defeated at almost every turn. Attis' shocking act of violence is not the poem's dramatic climax; rather, it initiates the action. Additionally, we may be surprised that Attis' motives are not explained more fully: why doesn't Catullus delve deeper into his psychology? The answer, I believe, is that Attis is not a three-dimensional character (in the modern literary sense), but, like many figures from the realm of myth, archetypal. He manifests – in the extreme – certain traits (mainly negative) associated in ancient culture with desirable young men. And while Catullus clearly disapproves of Attis' over-attachment to the role of *puer delicatus* ('tender boy') and his rejection of adult civic responsibility, poem 63 also betrays an anxious empathy with him. The pull of Cybele's savage power comes across in the feverish details Catullus gives of her rites. Though Catullus points out how Attis erred, he acknowledges his own fear of the goddess when he prays that she inflict her 'madness' elsewhere. He does not rule out the possibility that he, too, could fall prey to it.

Of the English reworkings of poem 63, the most singular is probably Leigh Hunt's dramatic monologue 'From Velluti to his Revilers'. In 1825, the Italian *castrato* singer Velluti appeared on stage in London, to the consternation of some members of the British public. Hunt's poem, a plea for greater tolerance, explicitly holds up Attis as a tragic figure and a counterpart to Velluti. Hunt's narrator ('Velluti') is made to meditate on Catullus' 'pale' verses about Attis, the 'poor bigot' (143-8; 151-2; 156-63):

> How often have I wept the dreadful wrong,
> Told by the poet in as pale a song,
> Which the poor bigot did himself, who spoke
> Such piteous passion when his reason woke! –
> To the sea-shore he came, and look'd across,
> Mourning his native land and miserable loss ...
> I see him, hear him, I myself am he,
> Cut off from thy sweet shores, Humanity! ...
> 'Twas ask'd me once (that day was a black day)
> To take this scene, and sing it in a play!
> Great God! I think I hear the music swell,
> The moaning bass, the treble's gibbering yell;
> Cymbals and drums a shattered roar prolong,
> Like drunken woe defying its own song:
> I join my woman's cry; it turns my brain;
> The wilder'd people rise, and chase me with disdain!

The play based on the Attis myth seems to have been Hunt's own invention, and it is an effective device, closely binding Velluti's predicament to that of his fellow sufferer. 'From Velluti to his Revilers' testifies to its author's careful, lively engagement with the text of Catullus 63. 'Velluti''s declaration, 'I see him, I hear him, I myself am [Attis]', grammatically recalls Attis' own statement at line 63, 'I have been a woman, I a young man, I an ephebe, I a boy'. In a neat twist, when Hunt's 'Velluti' imagines himself playing the part of Attis on stage he seems to hear the wild music of the orchestra, like that of Cybele's troupe ('it turns my brain'), and the disapproving British audience – in place of Cybele's lions – chase after him. Of course, a major point of divergence between the poems is that 'Velluti''s castration, unlike that of Attis, was not self-imposed.

Rather less melodramatic than Hunt's poem is a 1968 version of 63 by the American poet Robert Clayton Casto. For Casto – and for most of Catullus' readers today, I suspect – it is the sheer, illogical violence of the poem that resonates loudest. In the words of Casto's Cybele, the 'regent of Force', to her obedient lions (114-16),

> – Go chase him from the branches of the sea
> for he would dance and still be free:
> go drive him up: THERE IS NO REMEDY.

Though in mood and style it could not be further removed from 61, poem 63 does serve as that poem's thematic complement. It could almost be described as a mirror image of 61, representing the same features in inverted form. Both poems describe pivotal gender-related transitions: for the bride of 61, her passage from girlhood to matronhood; for Attis, the passage from ephebe to full-fledged adult male – alas, derailed. In 61, Iunia's transition is anchored by the mores and rituals of her Roman society; in 63, on the other hand, Attis' self-inflicted

94

change takes place, initially within a skewed society of the deranged, and ultimately in a social void. The bride's new role is one primarily of fecundity; Attis', of sterility, in his perverse 'marriage' to Cybele. Marriage and personal transition are themes that figure prominently, too, on the larger canvas of poem 64, Catullus' greatest achievement.

The Artist in a Fallen World

Relating the marriage of the mythical hero Peleus to the sea-nymph Thetis in no less than 408 hexameters (the metre of ancient epic), poem 64 is a *tour de force* that differs markedly from every poem discussed so far. Yet in the five hundred years since Catullus' work arrived in Britain, even his enthusiastic readers have been baffled by the poem. Few have tried their hands at translating it. One who did in the 1930s, the poet Basil Bunting, became frustrated (presumably) by its abstruse mythological and literary allusions, and its detailed 'back story', so uncharacteristic of Catullus' occasional pieces. After rendering the first 28 lines into a vigorous, alliterative English, Bunting gives up, deflating the epic style with a sharp aside (18-22):

> ... Peleus,
> to whom Jove the godbegetter, Jove himself yielded his mistress,
> for the sea's own child clung to you
>
> *– and why Catullus bothered to write pages and pages of this drivel mystifies me.*

Critics, too, have equivocated. None has denied the poem's virtuosity: 'magnificently extravagant' and 'a masterpiece' are judgments found in two recent books on Catullus.[1] But its elaborateness has led some to complain of a lack of depth in the way of personal emotion or moral purpose. Catullus came in for the harshest opprobrium on this count during the late nineteenth century. 'The poem is full of great beauties of detail; but as a whole it is cloying and yet not satisfying', proclaimed J.W. Mackail in his 1895 handbook on Latin literature, which was so popular that it went into a dozen reprints.[2] Two Latinists of the same era denounced poem 64 as 'artificial', and its centrepiece *ecphrasis* (see below) as 'out of all proportion to the rest'.[3] Even today, when such cavils are rarely voiced, poem 64 apparently still eludes, or daunts, Catullus scholars. To my knowledge, only two of the several English books on Catullus published since 1985 devote substantial space to the poem – though its length exceeds that of the first twenty-five of the polymetrics put together.

Here, I contend that poem 64 is a masterpiece of Latin literature, its intricacy not a symptom of dreaded 'artificiality', but a brilliant and satisfying display of the poet's powers. Catullus' engagement of visual paradigms throughout the poem pushes at the limits of conventional literary representation. Gorgeous verse, he seems to imply, may rival or even surpass the imagistic power (the effect on the 'mind's eye') of a work of visual art, such as a painting or statue-group. Moreover, artistic representation is linked throughout poem 64 to the idea of belatedness, that is, of art being removed from, or opposed to, original experience. (So, for instance, as successive generations of poets have drawn on their precursors to write about the gods, they have moved further and further away from the time when the gods were immanent.) What follows is a detailed discussion of the poem with a special emphasis on its relation to visual experience.

Genre and structure

Poem 64 is often labelled an *epyllion*, or 'miniature epic', but this term was coined only in the nineteenth century. There is no evidence for what Catullus' contemporaries might have called such a work (if not simply *epos*, an epic). Whatever its ancient name, the *epyllion* enjoyed a vogue at Rome during the middle of the first century BC. We know of a number of modish young writers of Catullus' era who composed scaled-down, epic-style Latin poems: in his poem 95 Catullus praises the *Zmyrna* (now lost) by his friend Cinna, designating it a 'little monument' and contrasting it favourably to Volusius' ponderous *Annales*. And other ancient sources mention an *Io* by Catullus' good friend Calvus and a *Glaucus* by Cornificius (the addressee of poem 38). These titles, and the few fragments that have come down to us, suggest that the late Republican neoteric poets favoured obscure mythological subjects and cultivated a style more subjective than that of full-length epic. In this they followed the innovative Hellenistic poets Callimachus and Theocritus.

A good indication of Catullus' likely model – or models – for 64 is what remains of Callimachus' short epic *Hecale*, whose story can be reconstructed as that of Theseus' journey to fight the Bull of Marathon; Callimachus apparently made the old woman Hecale, not Theseus, the central figure in his poem. Since Catullus' *epyllion* is the only complete example that survives, however, we cannot help but compare it to long epics such as the *Odyssey* and Apollonius of Rhodes' *Argonautica*, which, moreover, the poet self-consciously brings into play in his own work.

Poem 64 is a story-within-a-story. The 'outer' story involves the love at first sight and marriage of two figures from mythology, Peleus (a Greek hero, one of the crew of Jason's ship *Argo*) and Thetis (a Nereid or sea-nymph). The poem's 'inner' story relates an episode from the myth of Theseus, the Minotaur-slayer, and Ariadne, the Cretan princess who helps him escape from the beast's labyrinth. Catullus writes of

Theseus' desertion of Ariadne on the island of Naxos, and her subsequent rescue by the god Bacchus, by means of a literary device known as *ecphrasis*, an elaborate set-piece description of a work of visual art. (Famous *ecphraseis* include Homer's description of the shield of Achilles in *Iliad* 18.) In Catullus' poem, the art object is a rich purple coverlet embroidered with scenes from the Theseus-Ariadne myth; draped over the marriage-couch of Peleus and Thetis, the coverlet deftly connects the 'inner' and 'outer' stories.

The basic structure of poem 64 can be broken down as follows:

The Age of Heroes and the marriage of Peleus and Thetis	1-49
The Coverlet – Ariadne on Naxos; Theseus and Aegeus; Iacchus' orgies	50-264
Departure of mortal wedding guests; arrival of the gods; the Fates	265-322
Song of the Fates	323-381
Conclusion – the corruption of the present age	382-408

Already we can see that the *ecphrasis* on the coverlet comprises 214 lines, more than half of the poem's total. In traditional long epic, *ecphraseis* are relatively brief digressions, placed so as to adorn the primary narrative; in poem 64, however, the description of the coverlet may be said to outweigh the 'main' (outer) story of Peleus and Thetis, thereby subverting the conventions of the epic genre – and the expectations of Catullus' readers. The poet's unorthodox handling of *ecphrasis* has been seen as perverse ('out of all proportion to the rest'), but it is better regarded as a challenge to the idea that description must be incompatible with, or subordinate to, action. Catullus expands the possibilities of ecphrastic narrative in poem 64.

Because the poem continuously engages in dialogue with the visual arts, its overall structure can be conceived of visually. We can discern that the outer narrative 'frames' the inset *ecphrasis* and also the Song of the Fates. The *ecphrasis* itself incorporates various smaller elements: Ariadne's lament; Theseus' tragic return to Athens; Aegeus' lament; and Iacchus' (i.e. Bacchus') search for the abandoned Ariadne. Readers might visualise the components of the whole poem arranged as such:

Theseus and Ariadne on Crete	Aegeus' speech to Theseus	
Iacchus and followers	Ariadne on Naxos	Theseus' return to Athens (death of Aegeus)

Note that there are two episodes inset into the coverlet itself, and therefore doubly removed from the 'main' narrative – these are the history of Ariadne and Theseus' love-affair (76-123) and the speech by Aegeus, King of Athens and Theseus' father (212-37). These episodes occur before the action of both the outer *and* inner stories. (Of course they must predate the Peleus-Thetis story if the wedding guests see these episodes represented on the coverlet. But even within the Theseus-Ariadne myth they come before Ariadne's abandonment on Naxos.) So what seems to recede into the background in the diagram also, within the poem's timescale, recedes further into the mythic past. I will return to the diagram later in this chapter, after examining the poem in greater detail.

6. The Artist in a Fallen World

Mythic beginnings

The Hellenistic poets Callimachus and Apollonius, in common with the rest of the Greek poetic 'school' that flourished in Alexandria during the third century BC, devoted much of their verse to the exploration of origins: the origins of cults, rituals, cities, and so on. This preoccupation with aetiology (from the Greek *aetia*, 'origins') is manifest in poem 64. Catullus begins his *epyllion* with an account of the origins of the Argo, said to have been the world's first ship (1-11):

> Pine-trees born long ago on the peak of Mt Pelion
> Are said to have swum through Neptune's clear waves
> To the surf of Phasis and the borders of Aeetes,
> When chosen men, the oaks of Argive youth,
> Keen to seize a golden pelt from the Colchians,
> Dared to overtake salt shallows in a swift stern,
> Stroking caerulean plains with palms of fir.
> For these men the goddess protecting high city-ramparts
> Herself made a chariot to fly with the light wind,
> Joining latticed pine to bent keel.
> Its prow steeped raw Amphitrite in voyaging.

In this dazzling display of his verbal ingenuity, Catullus recounts the maiden voyage of the original ship, the *Argo*, condensing the relevant details of the legendary quest for the Golden Fleece into a mere eleven lines. From this brief introduction we learn that the *Argo* – constructed by the goddess Athena ('the goddess protecting high city-ramparts') from the pines of Mt Pelion (in Thessaly), and equipped with 'palms' (oars) of fir – sailed to the 'borders of Aeetes' (Colchis, modern Georgia, where Aeetes was king), its Argive crew seeking the 'golden pelt'. Catullus' account is bewildering without some explication. Not only is it densely allusive, referencing Apollonius, Euripides and Ennius, it supplies the background details in a seemingly illogical order. For instance, Catullus tells us that pine-trees 'are said to have swum' through the ocean before he even mentions the *Argo*. Yet this unusual narrative strategy creates a striking visual effect: like a tracking shot in a film, our 'view' of the poetic landscape sweeps from the heights of Mt Pelion down to the sea and across to the Colchian coast – all in a matter of three verses.

Catullus forges a mannered style through his ingenious use of figurative language. His metaphor in line 4, 'oaks of Argive youth', is another rhetorical flourish and forms a nice comple-ment to the animate pines and firs of lines 1-2 and 7. 'Its prow steeped raw Amphitrite in voyaging' (11) is an abstruse way of saying, 'The *Argo* introduced the sea to seafaring' (Amphitrite was Neptune's wife, and represented the sea). But line 11 is significant for another reason. Catullus' assertion – that the *Argo* 'steeped' (literally), or 'accustomed' the sea to maritime activity – runs counter to our expectations. Wouldn't the *sea*, rather, teach the inexperienced mariners to beware its raw power? In this first of many gestures toward the opposition between nature and art, the poem suggests that human innovation can get the better of natural forces, at least some of the time.

Picking up this same thematic thread is a word that occurs in line 15, 'marvel' or 'prodigy' (*monstrum*). (The Latin word had a negative tinge, like its English equivalents 'monster' and 'monstrous'.) Here, one 'marvel', the ship, immediately gives way to another: the incredulous Nereids, or sea-nymphs, rise out of the water to see the ship, exposing their bodies to the eyes of mortals (specifically, the Argonauts) for the first time. Peleus and Thetis instantly fall in love, and – for the first time – a mortal weds an immortal nymph. Countering the negative overtones of *monstrum* is Catullus' salute to the heroes as 'a race of Gods' in lines 22-3b. By committing a marvellous or prodigious act, Peleus wins (deservedly, the poet implies) a nymph's love and the grudging admiration of Jove himself.

The love and betrothal of Peleus and Thetis is dispensed with briefly in lines 19-21. Nevertheless it may bring to mind another great prodigy: the most famed hero of the Trojan War, Achilles, Peleus and Thetis' son. Achilles may be said to embody the equivocal value of *monstrum* on account of his wondrous yet terrifying feats in battle. His absent presence in poem 64 sits uneasily with Catullus' description of the joyous wedding guests arriving at Peleus' palace in lines 31-7. 'They declare their joy in their faces', we are told of the country people (line 34). Yet this happiness is deceptive. Thessaly's farmers have abandoned their labours and flocked to the palace in droves, and as a result, the countryside sinks into utter disorder (38-9, 42):

> No one tends the fields, the necks of the oxen grow soft;
> No crouching vine is weeded with curved hoes ...
> Foul rust attacks the abandoned ploughs.

Catullus upsets the idyllic nuptials with his encroaching weeds and rust, emblems of decay. Far from being the Islands of the Blessed, where the Greek poet Hesiod says the great heroes of myth dwell – and where the bounteous earth offers up 'honey-sweet fruits' – poem 64's Thessaly is already suffering the hardships of Hesiod's Age of Iron. (In his *Works and Days*, Hesiod lays out the five ages of mankind: Golden, Silver, Bronze, Heroic, and Iron. With the exception of the Heroic Age – a brief, happy respite – the ages become progressively debased.) Catullus' poem seems to anticipate the transition between the Heroic and Iron Ages, which coincided with the fall of Troy, whose fate was sown at the union of Peleus and Thetis.

Beholding desire

Shortly before he presents the wedding-bed coverlet to eager eyes, Catullus primes our visual imagination with a vivid description of the Thessalian palace. In contrast to the rust and choking weeds of the countryside, this urban vista is resplendent with gold, silver and ivory. The vocabulary Catullus employs in lines 43-9 ('shine', 'glows', 'gleam') is that of the visual arts, and may have a special relation to Roman Second Style wall-painting: much as the gleaming palace in 64 is said to have 'receded' from the peasants' view, the landscapes portrayed in frescoes from the mid to late first century BC also stretch backwards, features in the distance appearing ever higher and smaller.[4] As William Fitzgerald has observed, the contrast between rural rust and urban gold is another ironic twist on the literary ideal of the Golden Age; rather than remain on their farms to enjoy nature's bounty, these Thessalians linger in the city to feast their eyes on man-made opulence.

And we feast our eyes, too, on the palace structure itself, on the thrones and royal treasure, and then – when the poet directs our gaze toward it – on Thetis' wedding-couch, draped with a purple coverlet. Our gaze focusses on the 'ancient figures' (50) embroidered there, and on one in particular: Ariadne standing on the shore of Naxos, gazing after faithless Theseus as he sails away, leaving her alone. In a masterly chain of negative constructions, the poet then sweeps the reader's eyes over the girl's body, and her beautiful garments that have fallen away. We visualise, almost simultaneously, Ariadne first attired in these clothes before her lover's departure, then disrobed and grieving. She watches Theseus' ship from the beach (63-7),

6. The Artist in a Fallen World

Not keeping the finely-worked cap on her golden head,
Not covered by thin fabric draped on her chest,
Not cinched around the milky breasts by a smoothed band –
All of which had slipped off her body haphazardly
And at her feet the salt waves were playing with them.

As the ship disappears over the horizon, Catullus' tale slips back further into the past, to the time of Theseus' arrival on Crete. The story of Theseus and the Minotaur is one of the best known of classical mythology. In the most common version of the myth, Minos, the king of Crete, demanded an annual tribute from the rival state Athens of seven young men and seven maidens, to be sacrificed to the Minotaur (a monstrous man-bull). Theseus, Prince of Athens, decided to kill the Minotaur and so relieve his people of the harsh tribute. He travelled to Crete and met the princess Ariadne, who fell in love with him, and gave him a crucial aid in his task: a ball of string, which he unwound as he made his way through a labyrinth into the Minotaur's lair, and then used to retrace his path after slaying the beast.

Turning away now from this 'background' story of Ariadne and Theseus on Crete, Catullus returns to the 'foreground' depiction of Ariadne on the beach at Naxos. Again, our eyes are encouraged to linger on her physical form, as she runs bare-legged into the surf and displays her tear-stained face. At line 132 she begins a long monologue, a simultaneously pathetic and vengeful lament, the kind of discourse with which the archetypal abandoned woman has been associated throughout the history of Western literature (and music: operatic arias are often sung by abandoned women, including Ariadne herself in Richard Strauss' *Ariadne auf Naxos*). Though he did not invent the tradition of the abandoned woman's complaint (there are Greek precedents), Catullus was instrumental in developing it.

Many elements of Ariadne's monologue will be familiar to readers, even to those who have never encountered Catullus' poem before. Anyone who has read Dido's speech in *Aeneid* 4 or Sappho's lyrics – or Tennyson's 'Mariana', or Sylvia Plath's 'Daddy' – will recognise some of its salient features. Ariadne bewails Theseus' falsity and thoughtlessness. Ruefully, she recalls how eloquent he was: with 'smooth speech' (139-40) he made promises that later proved to be empty, so empty that 'light winds tore them, vain, all apart' (142). (Note the correspondences with two of the Lesbia poems, 70 and 76: 'What a woman says to an ardent lover / Ought to be written on the wind and on flowing water', 70.3-4; 'But entrusted to an ungrateful heart, all [my kindnesses] have been wasted', 76.9.) Next, Ariadne reflects on the proverbial unkindness of men to women they have seduced and grown weary of. She then considers the particular obligation owed her by Theseus. She rescued Theseus from the Minotaur's labyrinth, and in return she has been left to die alone on Naxos, where her unburied corpse will be carrion for vultures – a fate that the ancients believed denied one's soul peace after death. In the patronage-based society of Republican Rome, the principle of mutual obligation was held inviolable; for Theseus to renege on his debt to the woman who saved his life would likely have struck Catullus' contemporaries as, indeed, unnatural – but romantic relationships were not necessarily governed by the values of patronage, as certain of the elegiac poems (discussed in Chapter 7) make clear.

Clearly, Ariadne's speech is not to be understood as realistic. No woman in her predicament would actually deliver fluent hexameter verses into the void. Rather, the speech is a brilliant demonstration of the powers of rhetoric, which can not only stall but undermine epic action. 'Ariadne functions not to speed the plot', remarks Lawrence Lipking, 'but to drag against it, to remind and remind and remind us of what is left out [of the main wedding narrative] …. She will not stop lamenting.'[5] The surprising force of her rhetoric – which, though only one woman's, succeeds within the poem's timeframe in delaying Achilles' birth and thus impedes the build-up to the Trojan War – crystallises in lines 158-63:

> If our marriage hadn't been to your liking,
> Because you feared the harsh strictures of your old father,
> You could have at least taken me to your home
> So that I, as a slave, might have waited on you in pleasant
>   labour,
> Soothing your white soles in flowing water
> Or covering your bed with a purple quilt.

Ariadne has availed herself of every rhetorical strategy known to abandoned women (her literary sisters) – perhaps above all, the conventional complaint about the deceitful glibness of the lover. But this complaint is undercut by her meta-literary allusion to the purple coverlet at line 163. If we did not understand before, we see now that Ariadne's lament is pre-eminently a work of art. Catullus' self-referencing language (he uses almost exactly the same words for 'purple coverlet' here, *purpurea vestis*, as he does at lines 49-50) brings the artistry of the poem into sharp relief.

It is interesting, too, that Ariadne should conjure up, in her mind's eye, a purple coverlet. As we gaze in our imaginations on the sad scene at Naxos, she, the object of our gaze, in turn pictures a longed-for scene of domestic bliss with Theseus, in which visually beautiful things (the white soles of Theseus' feet, contrasted against the purple fabric) stand out. Note the importance of the act of looking in this section of Catullus' poem, and the next section. We look at Ariadne looking after the fleeing Theseus, who is eagerly looked *for* by his father, Aegeus. Tellingly, when the king bids farewell to Theseus in Athens, he confesses that his 'dimming *eyes* are not yet sated with [his] son's beloved form' (219-20); he instructs his son, 'when your eyes first *discern* our hills' of Athens (233), to hoist white sails, 'so that *seeing*, I may learn your joy with a glad mind' (236-7). But Theseus forgets his father's words, and Aegeus, spying the black sails that falsely proclaim his son's death, throws himself off the Acropolis.

Equally significant as looking here is the act of forgetting. The Latin adjective for 'forgetful'/'thoughtless' (*immemor*), and the verb 'to forget' (*obliviscor/oblitus*), appear multiple times in both Ariadne's lament and the account of Theseus and Aegeus. 'Heroes tend to be forgetful of those they are supposed to love', Lipking notes, 'but abandoned women will not let them forget with impunity'.[6] Sure enough, Ariadne calls on the Furies to avenge her mistreatment. With 'the same mind' with which he deserted her, Ariadne implores, may Theseus 'bring death on himself and his kin' (200-1). That her words hit home reminds us of the conventional use of black magic by abandoned women, particularly by witches like Medea. What Ariadne wishes on Theseus is the tragic – perhaps inevitable? – outcome of his own thoughtlessness. More than anything, she wants Theseus to know how it feels to be left behind by one you love (in his case, Aegeus), and the painful guilt of having forgotten about that person.

'But in another part ...' (251) of the coverlet, Iacchus (Bacchus) makes his way toward Ariadne with his company of satyrs and thyads (also known as maenads, ecstatic female worshippers). Catullus redirects our focus from the scene of Theseus' return to Athens, to this discrete vignette – I think of it as being on the far-left side of the coverlet, 'behind' the unsuspecting Ariadne (see diagram on p. 100). It is rich in visual detail: we watch the frenzied thyads shake their heads, brandish *thyrsi* (wooden staffs topped with pine-cones), throw around the dismembered limbs of a cow in a Bacchic rite, and wrap themselves with coiling snakes. There are specific sonic details, too. Iacchus' troupe plays tambourines, cymbals, horns, and pipes. Readers can't hear the music, though line 260 teases us with it: when some of the god's cohorts flock to secret rituals (*orgia*), Catullus coyly describes them as 'Those mysteries the profane desire, vainly, to hear'. Just as Catullus challenges the poetic hierarchy that holds ecphrasis inferior to epic action, here he may be hinting that lush poetic description can substitute for sound as well as for sight. Conversely, however, he may be exposing the limitations of his medium. For us – the poet's audience in the Age of Iron – a full and immediate experience of the mythic events is out of reach. As 'fallen' readers, we must rely on Catullus' poem, a virtuoso representation of myth but a *representation* nonetheless.

Like us, the countryfolk in the palace who gaze at the coverlet are excluded from firsthand experience of the world of myth. Ironically, at this most prodigious union of a nymph with a mortal man, the people of Thessaly do not interact with the divine wedding guests – they swiftly disband to make way for the arriving gods. Their retreat contradicts the happy picture of divine-mortal harmony in lines 251-64, where the human Ariadne and maenads freely, joyously intermingle with immortal Bacchus and his immortal satyrs. As the Thessalians would have known, Ariadne enjoyed a semi-apotheosis at the hands of her second, divine lover: in some ancient tellings of the myth, Bacchus takes Ariadne's wreath and sets it in the sky as a constellation ('the crown'). The scorned – or fallen – woman is redeemed. No divine fate lies in store for the Thessalians, we gather. When they are sated with looking on the coverlet, they go back home to their overgrown fields and rusted ploughs.

Spinning time's thread

But the gods do not have to content themselves with mere looking. After they settle into 'snow-white seats' (thrones made of ivory), and the banqueting tables before them are heaped with an 'abundant feast', the night's entertainment begins. As at a typical Greek or Roman wedding, this consists of music, specifically, an epithalamium. We know from poems 61 and 62 that epithalamia (or at least some of their parts and refrains) were sung by choruses of young women and men; musical performance at ancient weddings seems to have been a group affair. In poem 64, the gods also follow this custom, watching and listening to a group perform a wedding hymn. However, in place of Apollo and the Muses, who undertake this task in other versions of the myth, there are three wizened hags – the Parcae, or Fates. Personifications of the abstract concept of *fatum* – which determined the broad outline of one's life and death – the Parcae were conceived of as elderly women, continually spinning the threads of mortal fate (a person's life was sometimes envisaged as a 'thread' that the Parcae would spin, and then cut at its destined end).

William Fitzgerald suggests that Catullus' choice of the Parcae to deliver Peleus and Thetis' epithalamium presents an ironic contrast to the nubile girls who performed erotic dances at aristocratic banquets in Rome. Certainly the language Catullus uses to describe the Parcae is more commonly applied to attractive young women. Just as he lingered over the image of Ariadne standing naked on the beach, he now itemises every detail of the singers' less pleasing appearance (307-10; 316-17):

> A plain white garment, wrapping around the shaky body,
> Encircled the ankles with a purple hem,
> And rose-coloured headbands sat on the snowy crowns,
> As their hands dutifully plucked at the perpetual task ...
> Bitten-off wool clung to their chapped, thin lips,
> Which before had gummed the fine yarn.

With their trembling bodies tightly sheathed in their gowns, red fillets (headbands) incongruously placed on their venerable white heads, and tufts of wool sticking to their dry lips, Catullus' Parcae border on the grotesque. In fact, the borderline grotesque seems to be the prevailing mode of the Parcae's song, which foretells the awesome deeds of the newlyweds' future son, Achilles. In the brief (58-line) epithalamium, Catullus has the Parcae conjure four Trojan scenes as visually striking as they are appalling.

First, the Parcae say, the witnesses to Achilles' heroic feats will be – not his vanquished enemies, or the admiring gods, but the bereaved mothers of the men he has slain. In what may be a distorted reflection of the image of disconsolate Ariadne, these mothers let down their long (white) hair, and with their (feeble) hands beat their (sagging) breasts. Secondly, in a gorgeous, ironic simile, Catullus compares the slaughtering Achilles to a farmer reaping his harvest. The Greek hero 'will strike down' (355) the bodies of Trojan soldiers with his sword, like a reaper taking his sickle to a field of corn-ears. The juxtaposition of the images is striking, and so is the irony of it – for the act of reaping is part of the agricultural cycle, in which death (winter) always gives way to renewed life (summer), but Achilles' carnage is just that, carnage: there will be no second Troy.

The last two scenes presented by the Parcae in their wedding song confirm this interpretation. Another witness to Achilles' deeds will be the river Scamander (in Phrygia), they predict, on which the hero is destined to inflict violence: 'choking' (359) its course with dead bodies, Achilles will 'warm up' (360) the water by mixing blood into it. The final witness to his dreadful might will be the 'snowy limbs of a felled virgin', the Trojan princess Polyxena, whose sacrifice is demanded by the ghost of Achilles at the end of the war (in Euripides' tragedy *Hecuba*). In the next strophe of their song, the Fates liken the dying Polyxena to 'an animal victim succumbing to the two-edged blade ... on bent knee, a headless body' (369-70).

Polyxena's bloody death on the burial mound of Achilles chillingly suggests the bloodletting of the bride (Thetis or Ariadne) on her wedding night. (Significantly, Polyxena herself was to be the bride of Achilles in the underworld.) Catullus' picture of the sacrificed virgin, though more shocking, serves the same function as the references to adultery in poem 61: it acknowledges the dangers surrounding the marriage at hand. But in the context of a 'mini-epic', the Polyxena passage also forces us to notice one particularly tragic victim of Achilles' heroic campaign. In this respect it is equivalent to Ariadne's lament, a reclaiming of the figures excluded from, or marginalised in, traditional epic narratives.

Following on from the rhetorical (and visual) power of Ariadne's lament, the Parcae's ambivalent epithalamium prompts us to ask whether Catullus is interrogating the concept of a morally good Heroic Age, versus the fallen modern condition. Were the Argonauts any better than the heroes of the Trojan War, and were either of them any better than we –

Catullus' readers – are? I do not regard the poem as a negative appraisal of morality in either first-century BC Rome or the Archaic Greece of legend. Rather, Catullus offers us a finely-wrought and subtle exploration of perspective, of what it means to look at art – or history or myth – and judge it as a spectator. The project of the poem as a whole, it could be argued, is to confront the sights that epic overlooks: abandoned women, casualties of war, the fact that individual lives are inexorably tethered to a greater destiny (thus at line 382 Peleus' happiness is said to lie, solely it seems, in his son's future feats in battle).

However, in the moralising epilogue that comprises the final twenty-six lines of the poem, Catullus contrasts the close inter-action of gods and mortals in past ages to the gods' withdrawal from human affairs in corrupt modern times. While religion was honoured, he writes, the gods would grace the rites performed for them on earth; but now they visit us no longer, since 'the welter of right and wrong, confused by our evil madness, has turned the gods' just intentions away from us' (405-6).

As has often been argued, the socio-political circumstances of Catullus' Roman world provide relevant context for the epilogue. The decade of the poet's birth witnessed the bloody upheaval of Rome's first civil war, between the rival generals Gaius Marius and L. Cornelius Sulla; when he emerged the winner, Sulla proceeded to massacre his enemies and confis-cated lands and goods from thousands of families (including many who were not even allied with Marius). Sulla's march on Rome in 88 BC and his subsequent dictatorship flagrantly violated Rome's Republican traditions, and set the stage for a second civil war, arising from Julius Caesar and Gnaeus Pompey's power-struggle a few years after Catullus' death. Although poem 64 cannot be reduced to a political allegory, Catullus' grim observation in 399 that 'Brothers washed their hands in brothers' blood' was especially true of his own life-time. Yet poem 64's sweeping canvas presents degradation as the constant plight of humanity, for whom the past is always golden, and never achievable.

7

The Elegiacs

Unfortunately, there is not space in this volume to consider poems 65, 66 and 67. These poems, along with 68 (discussed below), straddle the second and third sections of Catullus' corpus: like 61-64 they are of substantial length, but there is a significant formal difference – they are composed in the elegiac metre (of alternating hexameter and pentameter lines). None of poems 1-64 is written in this metre, but poems 65-116 are exclusively elegiacs. While there are a substantial 47 poems in this third section – rivalling the 58 polymetrics – many are only four lines in length or shorter.[1]

The majority of the elegiacs are epigrams, built around the stark antitheses and deflating final-verse 'punchlines' typical of that form. By turns these poems exhibit indignation, reproach and self-pity. Many are directed at obnoxious acquaintances: there is Rufus, whose goatish body odour drives all the girls away (poems 69 and possibly 77); 'Mentula' ('Prick') or Mamurra, who in his insatiable greed runs through the bounty of his large estate like a 'huge menacing prick' (115, also 94, 105 and 114); and Gellius, whose crime is 'impious coupling' with his mother and aunt (poems 74, 80, 88-91).

Gellius

The real-life target of Catullus' seven epigrams on Gellius seems to have been one L. Gellius Publicola (though the final name is doubtful), the son of a consul, who according to the first-century AD anthologist Valerius Maximus was rumoured to have inflicted a 'sexual disgrace' on his own stepmother (*Memorable Doings and Sayings* 5.9.1). It is for breaking both the law against adultery and the taboo against incest, and for adopting the shameful role of pathic (or passive) homosexual, that Catullus excoriates Gellius in poems 74, 80 and 88.[2]

The idea of Priapic punishment, mentioned above in connection with poem 16, is also highly relevant here. Again, Catullus-the-narrator is the virile male in control; however, instead of threatening to rape his victim personally (as in 15 and 16), he opts for a different approach, recounting Gellius' perverse and degrading sexual activity with others in order to paint him as weak. 'To expose victims as sexually abnormal – men as pathic homosexuals, women as promiscuous – is to imply sexual power over them, to threaten them as Priapus threatens thieves,' writes Richlin.[3] Furthermore, by detailing the specific sex acts that Gellius performs (in contrast to 16, where Aurelius and Furius are simply called 'fag' and 'pansy'), Catullus engages a concept that Richlin calls staining. The Romans had a horror of defiling the mouth, and consequently of all oral-genital contact; in the poems on Gellius discussed below, the loss of power that humiliates the fellator is compounded by befoulment.

74, the first epigram in the series, introduces Gellius and his incestuous tendencies. Catullus tells how Gellius flouted his uncle's strict standards of conduct – by seducing his uncle's own wife. Strangely, though, Catullus does not express any outrage at Gellius' behaviour. Not only does he not condemn him, he seems to relish the man's brazenness, as the obscene twist at the end of poem suggests:

7. The Elegiacs

Gellius had heard that Uncle would scold
Anyone who talked or behaved sexily.
So that this wouldn't happen to him, he rubbed down Uncle's
    wife,
And turned Uncle into Harpocrates.
He got what he wanted: for even if he made Uncle now
Suck it himself, Uncle wouldn't say a word.

To make sure that his uncle won't carp at him for his 'naughty habits', *deliciae* – the same erotically, and aesthetically, charged word found in poems 2, 3 and other of the polymetrics – Gellius hits on a sly idea. By seducing his uncle's wife, he makes his uncle into a cuckold, a figure of fun in many Roman texts. In a patriarchal society such as Rome's, where masculinity and social status are mutually reinforcing, a wife's adultery may be interpreted as a sign that the husband is not sufficiently powerful to control his wife (= women in general, and by implication also male social inferiors).

Presumably, Gellius' uncle in poem 74 is so humiliated by his wife's misbehaviour that, instead of divorcing her or seeking punishment against Gellius ('manly' courses of action), he will suffer it in silence. Gellius' act of incest 'turned Uncle into Harpocrates' – an Egyptian boy-deity represented in art holding one finger to his lips. Even in the face of such an insult to his manhood, Gellius' uncle remains silent, rather than expose himself to ridicule. He is so passive, Catullus implies, that he wouldn't speak up even if Gellius orally raped *him*. The joke, of course, is that Uncle wouldn't be able to speak with his mouth full.

For a poem initiating a series of attacks on Gellius, poem 74 unexpectedly takes aim at a different target – Gellius' uncle. After all, the immoral Gellius 'got what he wanted': the freedom to indulge in *deliciae* without being reprimanded by his (now-silenced) uncle. Catullus seems vicariously to enjoy Gellius' Priapic conquest. The epigram's final couplet pictures Gellius in the ultimate power display of the Roman male, forcing another man – his elder, and his uncle no less – to submit to him sexually. A single primary obscenity in line 5, *irrumare*, delivers a powerful jolt.[4]

The success of poem 74 as a humorous epigram depends on whether Catullus can get us to join him in mocking Gellius' uncle. He needs to convince us in six short verses that this humiliated man is deserving of ridicule. Richlin, drawing on Freudian theory, explains the relationship shared by joke-teller, joke-victim and audience thus: 'When A, the teller, tells a tendentious joke to C, the listener, about a victim B, A buries criticism by bringing C over to his side through laughter. A has done C a favor by breaking down in an acceptable way his barriers against expressing hostility … jokes thus become a sort of group reassurance.'[5] And in this case, it seems to me, Catullus is effective at bringing us over to his side, for two reasons. First – crucially – he positions the reader as his confidante. This is in marked contrast to poem 16, for instance, where the opening threat in the second person ('I'll ramrod you …') forces the reader into an uncomfortable identification with the poet's victims. But here, the third-person narration ('Gellius had heard …) signals that the audience will be safe from attack.

Second, any sympathy the reader might have for Gellius' uncle is compromised by the fact that he is a hypocrite. The same man who zealously denounces his acquaintances for their small liberties is strangely silent when it comes to a far more serious crime in his house, adultery – involving his own wife and nephew. His failure to adhere to the standard he sets for others recalls the proverbial wisdom of poem 22, where Catullus observes of an enthusiastic but talentless versifier: 'Each person's stuck with his peculiar failing,/ But we can't see the sack we're carrying (20-1)'. So, while the uncle's come-uppance at the end of 74 is shockingly explicit (and to some minds offensive, no doubt), it does have an ironic appropriateness, which is sharpened by the opposition that frames the poem: Uncle's past of self-righteous sermonising (lines 1-2) versus his current shamed silence (5-6).

In the next instalment in the series, poem 80, Gellius is consigned to a more negative and distinctly un-Priapic role – that of fellator. No moral violation such as adultery is imputed to him now, only the loss of his masculine dignity on account of his 'stained' mouth:

> How do you explain, Gellius, why those rosy lips of yours
> Become whiter than winter snow
> When you leave home in the morning and when the waning
>   day's eighth hour
> Nudges you from gentle rest?
> I can't think what's going on. Does Gossip whisper truly, that you
> Devour great stretches of men's middle-parts?
> Yes, it's certain. Poor old Victor's broken loins proclaim it,
> And the mouth, stained with milky whey.

Adopting a pose of faux-naïveté, Catullus quizzes Gellius about a seemingly minor change in his appearance. The mock-earnestness of the poet's tone is underscored by diction associated with the Latin high style. In ancient epic and lyric texts, young, attractive persons of both genders are said to have rosy lips or mouths (Virgil describes Venus as speaking with a 'rosy mouth' [*Aeneid* 2.593]); *labellum*, a diminutive for 'lip' (*labrum*) that occurs in line 1, is used by Catullus of a smiling baby in the long lyric 61. There are more parodic touches of the literary high style. 'Whiter than winter snow' echoes a Homeric description of horses (*Iliad* 10.437). Similarly, the phrase '(from) gentle sleep' in line 4 has high-style parallels, for instance, at 63.44, when Attis wakes *de quiete molli* and repents her madness. The pseudo-formality of Catullus' conclusion at line 7 – 'Yes, it's certain' (*sic certe est*) – harks back to a very different context, poem 62, in which the poet confirms that the evening star has risen (*sic certest*, 8), the cue for the wedding-song contest to begin.

Cutting into the mock-pretensions of these lines is a colloquial and disingenuous avowal: 'I can't think what's going on' (or, more literally, 'Surely there's something the matter', 5). This signals that the real reason for Gellius' new look does not merit the lofty rhetoric of 1-4. But Catullus immediately takes up the high style again, evoking humour from the incongruous application of 'literary' language to a subject as low (in Roman eyes) as male-male fellatio. His 'innocent' question in line 6, '(You) Devour great stretches of men's middle-parts?', hilariously skirts around the very sex act it alleges. This verse does not include a single primary obscenity (though the verb *vorare* was often used in obscene contexts, and seems to puncture the lofty register here). By contrast, in the final couplet of poem 74, the joke depended on the strongly obscene verb *irrumare*.

Poem 80 positions its audience as eavesdroppers, inviting us to listen in on an ostensibly private conversation between Catullus and Gellius. And most readers will enjoy the dramatic irony, the suspicion that Catullus must be preparing a great put-down, or else why would he invite us to overhear? We quickly catch on that the high-style language must be comically at odds with the situation it describes. The act of eavesdropping necessarily entails some guilt – we know we aren't *supposed* to be listening – but in this case, the guilt is mitigated by the poet's good humour. He does not make his audience complicit in a vicious character-assassination; instead, his aim seems only to make Gellius blush – and readers laugh.

In poem 88, Catullus takes the same rhetorical elements used in 80 and 74 (the literary high style; graphic sexual imagery; a string of 'leading' questions) and turns them to a harsher denunciation of Gellius. The technique of question-and-answer, which provides a frame for poem 88 (as well as for 80), has important parallels in other varieties of Roman invective, as is clear from Pompeian graffiti and reports of popular songs and chants. Thus both Plutarch and Cicero give accounts of an incident in which the demagogue P. Clodius Pulcher (brother of the notorious Clodia) whipped his crowd of supporters into a rage against his enemy Pompey, by posing questions such as 'Who is the degenerate general?' and 'Who is killing the people with hunger?', to which the claque shouted back, 'Pompey!'. Compare the opening of poem 88:

> What does the man do, Gellius, who with mother and sister
> Itches and – his tunic cast aside – stays up all night?
> What does the man do who doesn't let his uncle be a husband?

The allegation of incestuous adultery made in poem 74 is developed with, significantly, a stronger emphasis on its incestuous dimension – now Gellius is sexually involved 'with mother and sister' (the latter being his mother's sister rather than his own, given the reference to his uncle in line 3). Rather than hold up the cuckolded uncle as a laughing stock, as he does in 74, Catullus sets his sights on Gellius here, blaming him for appropriating the role of husband in his uncle's marriage. These initial hints of sharper disapproval on the part of the narrator are reinforced by line 4's pointed query, addressed to the reader as much as to Gellius:

Do you know how great a crime he begets?

Here, as in 74, the speaker supplies the answer to his own question. In the earlier poem he affected to hesitate, and played down his own role in discovering the truth: 'Does Gossip whisper truly? … Yes, it's certain.' This time he immediately, devastatingly makes clear just how immoral Gellius' behaviour is:

> He begets, o Gellius, a crime so great that neither outermost
>   Tethys
> Nor Ocean, father of Nymphs, can wash it away.
> For there is no crime which he could proceed to,
> Not if, head down, he gorged on himself.

The hair-raising last verse ascribes to Gellius not merely a talent for performing fellatio, as in 80, but for performing auto-fellatio, which lies outside the bounds of normal sexual practice. What poem 88 implies is that auto-fellatio is a logical extension of incest: having sex with oneself and having sex with one's kin are varieties of the same abomination.

Juxtaposing the high-style mythologising of lines 5-6 ('neither outermost Tethys…') to this explicit picture of sexual deviancy, poem 88 rouses not a belly laugh but a nervous snigger. Catullus' use of the high style, though comically exaggerated, is not for the purpose of outright mockery, as at 80.1-4; his point – that incest is a gross violation of the moral code – is a serious one. At the same time, the symbolic, quasi-religious power of Ocean and Tethys is unsettled and 'stained' by close proximity to the obscene Gellius; we are left to imagine Gellius head-down in his own crotch, an image so profane and outrageous it seems to shift the whole poem onto the plane of the absurd. It is a joke, after all.

7. The Elegiacs

Lesbia

Catullus' elegiac poems on Lesbia comprise the greater part of the Lesbia cycle, notwithstanding the popularity of the kiss and sparrow poems. They are, like the Gellius epigrams, often bitingly critical of their subject; yet they lack the vein of absurd grotesquerie which characterises that series. They do not – disappointingly, to many readers – give us a clear picture of Lesbia, either, beyond what we have already learned of her promiscuity (poems 11 and 58) and her hot-and-cold demeanour towards Catullus (poems 7 and 8). Nor do we get any description of her physical appearance or personal circumstances, except that she is married. By contrast, the later Roman elegists detailed their mistresses' particular charms and inclinations (which were, however, largely conventional). Tibullus, for example, says that his Delia is devoted to the goddess Isis, conscientiously observing her rites (I.3), and he writes of her 'slender arms' and 'flaxen hair' (I.5.43-4).

The Lesbia elegiacs focus almost exclusively on Catullus' emotional responses to Lesbia's (mis)conduct, not the conduct per se – Catullus doesn't specify what Lesbia has done to cause him pain. Rather, he stresses the distance between his formerly affectionate love for her and the contemptuous lust he presently feels, which he links to her unspecified transgressions. Here, perhaps more than anywhere else in the corpus, Catullus gives us a version of events carefully calibrated to show himself in a sympathetic light, continually taking pains to guide his readers toward the 'right' response.

Take poem 75, for example. Addressing Lesbia, Catullus bitterly ascribes all his mental turmoil to her 'lapse' (*culpa*) – and we are left to wonder what it was.

My resolve has sunk this low, Lesbia, on account of your lapse,
And it has destroyed itself so thoroughly by its own steadfastness
That it couldn't wish you well now, even if you were perfect,
Nor could it stop loving you if you did anything and everything.

Yet we instantly recognise the sentiment: desire for another person can be intense, even when the desired person does not command our respect or even affection. Catullus sharpens the contrast between his desire and (lack of) affection for Lesbia with precise diction. *Bene velle* in line 3, meaning 'to wish [you] well', is an expression normally used of the feeling between friends, and might be translated as 'to be fond of' or even 'to like'. Its semantic distance from the Latin *amare*, whose principal meaning is 'to love (sexually)', is rather farther than what separates the English 'like' from 'love'.

If being fond of a person was often distinct in Roman eyes from sexual love, then respecting or cherishing someone was another emotion again. It is this feeling – *diligere* in Latin – that Catullus juxtaposes with *amare* in poem 72:

You once said that you knew only Catullus, Lesbia,
And you wouldn't embrace even Jove instead of me.
I loved you then, not just as an ordinary man loves his girlfriend,
But as a father cherishes his sons and sons-in-law.
Now I really know you. Though I burn more intensely,
You're much cheaper and flimsier to me regardless.
'How is that', you ask? Because such an offence drives me
To love more, but to care less.

Diligere is the word the poet uses of his principal feeling for Lesbia, and he makes its distance from *amare* all the more obvious by comparing his own role as lover to that of a father who 'cherishes' his sons and sons-in-law. (His reference to how the ordinary man 'cherishes' his girlfriend is possibly ironic – an ordinary man wouldn't associate *diligere* with romance, Catullus implies.) Poem 72 hinges on a series of polar oppositions set up between terms that, paradoxically, overlap: *diligere* as (not) experienced by the common crowd for their women, and *diligere* as experienced by a caring father, are set out as different entities; so, too, are *diligere* and *amare*, and *amare* and *bene velle* (line 8). As the poem's last line reveals, their relationship is one of inverse proportion – as sexual love grows, fondness wanes.

Also subtly distinguished are 'know' in line 1 (Latin *nosse*) and 'know', *cognoscere*, in line 5. *Nosse* here has the sexual overtones it was later to carry in Latin translations of the Bible: Lesbia 'knows' Catullus sexually. Catullus' knowledge of her is somewhat different. Although *cognoscere* too sometimes conveys a sexual meaning (as at 61.180, where matrons are described as 'well known' to their husbands), it more often means 'to learn' or 'to recognise'. As Kenneth Quinn remarks, the phrasing here is 'bitterly ambiguous, the context drawing out equally the sense "now I have found you out"'.[6]

In the first half of the twentieth century poems 75 and 72 were especially significant in the eyes of Catullus' interpreters, who took them as evidence that Catullus was striving – against the mores of his age – for a 'whole love', integrating sexual desire with deep affection. Frank Copley, for example, who translated Catullus in the 1950s, ventured that, 'Far more important than the identity and the personality of Lesbia, in fact, even more important than the identity and personality of Catullus himself … is the special and unique quality and nature of the love about which he wrote so many poems.' Copley takes Catullus' protestations at face value, and assumes that the unravelling of the affair is Lesbia's fault (as the poet claims at 75.1): 'she did not care for or even understand the unique quality of the love he offered her'.[7] Two commentators in 1908 came down even more firmly on the poet's side: 'Catullus mourns for the chivalrous love, changed through Lesbia's fault to vulgar passion', is Macnaghten and Ramsay's sympathetic reading of poem 72.[8]

The fierce contempt Catullus claims to feel now for Lesbia, his sense of outrage at her failure to live up to his ideal, might lead us to conclude that the 'real' Catullus' emotions ran deeper than the 'real' Lesbia's. It is important not to forget that we're only getting his side of the story. That Lesbia has been proved cheap while Catullus is a victim of his own 'steadfastness' is not an unbiased account, coming as it does from Catullus. However, it's the only account we have, and regardless of its degree of historical truth, it gains *narrative* support from other of the elegiac poems.

Probably the ultimate expression of the depth of Catullus' love (on this view) is poem 68B, a labyrinthine and densely allusive long poem in elegiac couplets. Whether 68B is the second part (after 68A) of a single, unified poem 68, or should stand by itself as an independent poem, is a question that continues to vex Catullus scholars; the arguments are largely too technical to recount here. For the purposes of this discussion, I regard 68B as a stand-alone poem, though with a close thematic relation to the preceding piece, which was possibly intended as a kind of 'cover letter' for it.

Rich in figurative language and crowded with the cast of Greek myth, 68B weaves the details of Catullus' love-affair with Lesbia into the fabric of high-style mythological elegy. (The poet's mistress is not explicitly named as Lesbia, but she is married, and has other lovers besides Catullus [135-46], so the identification seems fairly certain.) The poem is addressed to a man called Allius who has come to Catullus' aid;[9] in a string of extended similes the poet compares his friend's kindness to a mountain spring that quenches thirsty travellers, and the gentle breeze for which sailors pray after a storm, before, twenty-five lines later, he finally identifies Allius' generous act (67-76):[10]

> He laid open an enclosed field with a wide path,
> He gave a house to us and our mistress,
> In which we could exercise our mutual love,
> Where my bright goddess directed her soft footstep
> And set a glowing arch on the worn doorsill,
> Pressing down with a creaky sandal,
> As once, burning with love for her husband,
> Laodamia came to the house which Protesilaus
> Had begun – in vain, since the hallowed blood of a sacrificial
>   victim
> Had not yet appeased heaven's masters.

So Allius has provided a trysting-place for Catullus and his lover. Lesbia – or the woman we assume is Lesbia – has metamorphosed from the flirtatious girl of the opening sequence (and the sexual adventurer of poem 58) to a 'bright goddess', as befits a poem with lofty epic precedents. Later, the characterisation of the *puella* as divine was to become standard in Augustan love-elegy. In *Amores* 1.7, for instance, Ovid is consumed with guilt after beating his mistress (32): 'Diomedes was the first to strike a goddess; I was the next.'

Yet the vividly realised moment when Lesbia crosses the threshold also evokes the entry of a Roman bride into her new husband's house, now her family home. Her radiance (the poet calls her 'my light') is a conventional attribute of feminine beauty and of bridal beauty in particular: in 61, for instance, Catullus describes Junia as 'like a shining Asian myrtle' (21-2), and her face as 'shining like a blossom' (186). That Catullus depicts his rendezvous with Lesbia as a wedding night of sorts is clear.

However, the analogy is immediately ironised – or perhaps glamorised – by the digression that follows, on the mythical couple Laodamia and Protesilaus. In the *Iliad*, Protesilaus is the first to leap ashore upon the arrival of the Greeks at Troy; he is killed instantly, leaving his new wife Laodamia tearing at her cheeks in grief, in a house half-built. (Later accounts of the story blame Protesilaus' fate on his own failure to sacrifice to the gods before establishing his house.) The poet's comparison of himself and his mistress to the doomed Greek newlyweds is apt in the sense that both relationships are frustrated – Protesilaus and Laodamia's by the exigencies of war, Catullus and Lesbia's by her being married to someone else. For lines 143-6 indicate that the goddess has a husband:

> Yet she did not come to me guided by her father's hand
> Into a house scented with Assyrian perfume,
> But on a miraculous night she gave me stolen little presents,
> Lifted right out of her husband's very lap.

This short passage turns the nuptial imagery of 69ff. on its head, as a blunt reminder that, whatever he (or we) may fancy, Lesbia legally belongs to another, and her sexual relationship with the poet is viewed by the Roman state as a 'theft' Catullus commits against her husband. Contrary to the idea of the decadent Romans that is current in our popular culture, among the elite in Republican Rome adultery (though not uncommon) 'was not readily tolerated', Catharine Edwards observes; 'If it had been, Roman texts would not be so insistently preoccupied with it.'[11] Catullus' reference to the 'stolen little presents' that Lesbia conveys to him from 'her husband's very lap' is potent. Pushing against the Laodamia and Protesilaus simile, it aligns the poet and his mistress instead with another couple from the legend of Troy, Paris and Helen, whose illicit love – Paris 'steals' Helen from Sparta – sparks off the long, hard-fought war in the first place. The death of Protesilaus and Laodamia's inconsolable grief, the doomed adultery of Helen and Paris – these narratives counteract each other, yet they combine to imbue poem 68 with a shade of darkness. Darker still is the narrative strand concerning the recent death of the poet's brother, and Catullus' startling claim, 'With you our whole house is buried' (94). Adulterous love, though it may be 'miraculous', was depressingly barren for the Romans: Catullus could not propagate his *gens* while attached to a married woman, for even if she were to bear his children, they would not legitimately belong to his family.

Sterile love and its attendant metaphor of burial are also suggested by lines 109-18, where Laodamia's passion for Protesilaus is compared to a deep abyss dug by Hercules after performing his fifth labour (the Greek word Catullus uses for 'abyss', *barathrum*, had strong negative connotations). Linking together these diverse analogies is not a linear narrative, but the associative power of a place, 'Troy the obscene, cursed Troy' (99), the scene of Paris and Helen's ill-fated affair and the grave of so many men – including Catullus' brother, buried 'in faraway soil' (100).

68B is to say the least a difficult poem, and it has a disorienting effect on the reader; nothing in it holds still long enough for us to get a sense of poet's stance. Is it possible that he rejects this 'shared love' (69) with a woman he deems a goddess, whom he has chosen to commemorate in a lengthy poem? Perhaps to believe so is only wishful thinking that he was morally 'better' (to modern eyes) than his words imply. Does he allude to Paris and Helen to acknowledge his feelings of guilt, or does he in fact *collapse* the distinctions between sanctioned and forbidden

love? After all, Laodamia and Protesilaus' union, though a legitimate marriage, was not approved by the gods – hence its
disappointment.

Despite the obscurity of much of the poem, one thing is
clear: Catullus treats his love for Lesbia with relative seriousness
in 68B, compared to his handling of it in the polymetrics. The
shift is not lost on readers, and one popular explanation for it
has been chronological – that in 68B, Catullus starts to realise
that his feelings for Lesbia run deep. But he also sets himself up
to be disillusioned. The crucial passage is 135-40:

> And although she is not content with her one Catullus,
> We'll tolerate the odd thefts of a demure mistress,
> Lest we're too troublesome, as stupid men are.
> Oftentimes even Juno, the greatest of the heaven-dwellers,
> Has stifled her blazing rage at her husband's weakness,
> Discovering the many thefts of all-willing Jove.

For those who read the Lesbia poems as a sequential autobiography, this represents a turning point in the love-affair.
Catullus acknowledges that his 'goddess', his 'light', sees other
men, but rather than give vent to his outrage (as at poem 58, for
instance), he is determined to tolerate her 'thefts', lest he make
a nuisance of himself. His apparently earnest effort to accept
Lesbia's other lovers looks forward to poems like 72, where that
effort ends in failure. Of course, other of the Lesbia poems do
not fit so easily into the autobiography as 68B. Considerable
reshuffling of the poems is required to get the story straight; so
poem 51 and poem 11, for example, are often seen as corre-
sponding to the beginning and the end of the affair, irrespective
of their placement in the corpus.

A final note on poem 68B: at line 138 the poet compares

himself to Juno, wife of the god Jupiter, whose constant philandering provokes the goddess's ire. Once again, Catullus aligns himself with the feminine – with the figure of the spurned woman. Yet classical mythology abounds with Juno's acts of vengeance, too, most of them unfairly directed at the women her husband seduces or rapes. (Juno turns Io and Callisto into a heifer and a bear respectively, and plays a vengeful trick on Semele that results in the latter's death.) Instead of taking Catullus' real-life victimhood at Lesbia's hands for granted, then, we should bear in mind that Catullus was an artist and used the tropes of Greco-Roman literature *to portray himself* as betrayed. Furthermore, his self-identification with Juno may ironise his claim that he is willing meekly to abide Lesbia's 'thefts'. As Juno's presence here reminds us, a jealous lover can seldom keep quiet.

Poems 87, 109 and 76: acting in good faith

The most explicit statement Catullus makes regarding the seriousness of his love for Lesbia, however, is poem 87, which likens that love to one person's pledge, steadfastly upheld, in a two-way contract:

> No woman can truly say she's been loved so much
> As my Lesbia's been loved by me.
> No loyalty so great was ever found in any pact
> As was on my part, in my love for you.

Catullus' claim here is one of exceptionalism – the love he bears, or bore, Lesbia is unique in its intensity, and Lesbia in turn is unique in being the sole object of such a love. (How many lovers through history have declared, 'No one has loved another as

fiercely as I do!' The universality of the lover's claim to exceptionalism is, of course, ironic.) To add ballast to his words, the
poet draws an analogy, not with another grand passion (Paris
and Helen's, say), but with a social alliance from outside the
domain of romantic love. Catullus writes that his loyalty or
'good faith' (*fides*, whence the English 'fidelity') shown towards
his beloved has surpassed the good faith rendered by any other
person ever bound to a social contract, a *foedus*.

The idea, or more properly institution, of *foedus* was integral
to upper-class society in Republican Rome. Conducting business in Rome was not nearly so formal as it is in the modern
work-world; political and commercial alliances usually sprang
from personal relationships, and men saw to their affairs largely
in their own homes, where they were visited by their clients
(who were almost indistinguishable from family friends). In his
recent popular biography of Cicero, Anthony Everitt cogently
describes the clientship (*clientela*) system that was a pillar of
Roman society:

> A wealthy and powerful man acted as a 'patron' for many
> hundreds or even thousands of 'clients.' He guaranteed to look
> after their interests .... In return, a client (if he lived in Rome)
> would regularly pay a morning call and accompany his patron
> as he went about his business in town .... These networks of
> mutual aid cut across the social classes and linked the local
> elites in the various Italian communities, not to mention those
> in the Empire as a whole, to the center .... A family's client list
> survived from one generation to the next. Durable bonds
> could, of course, also be established between equals.[12]

In the context Everitt presents, a typical *foedus* would be a
personal, political or commercial association entered into by

friends whose families were already involved in a patron-client relationship (the clients in this system, incidentally, were not necessarily of low social standing; Cicero's family, rural gentry, were clients to some of the leading aristocrats in Rome). Though it is etymologically linked to *fides*, the word *foedus* has a more political flavour, and was often used of treaties made between Rome and her foreign dominions. As with Roman culture as a whole, the personal and political aspects of the *foedus* cannot be disentangled from one another.

When Catullus invokes his and Lesbia's *foedus* in poem 87, he alludes to the near-reverence in which such treaties traditionally were held at Rome. In a society which placed religion at the centre of the state apparatus, breaking a *foedus* – though it be only commercial – was cause for censure, an offence against right conduct (*virtus*). Catullus, by stressing his own strict adherence to the *foedus* in poem 87, implies that his behaviour was not reciprocated. Lesbia, therefore, would be guilty of a gross violation of the Roman social code.

Yet it seems unusual that Catullus should apply a political term like *foedus* to a love-affair, and an illicit love-affair with a married woman at that. *Foedus* is one of a handful of 'loaded' Catullan words that scholars classify together as, in R.O.A.M. Lyne's phrase, 'the language of aristocratic obligation'. What Lyne and others mean by this will be clear from the discussion above. Apart from *foedus* and *fides*, the words denoting this type of language include 'loyal friendship' (*amicitia*), 'conscientiousness' (*pietas*), 'service' (*officium*) and, on the other side of the moral coin, 'offence' (*iniuria*) and being 'ungrateful' (*ingratus*). Such words feature prominently in, for instance, poem 109 (my italics):

> My life, you suggest to me that this sweet love of ours
> Will endure between us forever.

133

Great gods, see that she's able to promise truly,
That she may say this earnestly and from her heart,
And that we may be allowed to maintain through our whole lives
This *eternal pact of hallowed friendship*.

Now that we have identified the language of so-called aristocratic obligation, the poem reveals itself as more than a
moping lover's *cri de coeur*. Far from being corny or insipid,
the final verse has a surprising ethical weight. Four 'loaded'
words are strung together: 'eternal', 'hallowed', 'pact' and
'friendship'. In Latin, the line has an unusually high number
of long, open vowel sounds such as 'ae' and 'oe' diphthongs
(*aeternum hoc sanctae foedus amicitiae*), which slow down the
pace, lending it gravity.

Yet for all this, there is something askew in Catullus' argument. Poem 109 proposes an equivalence between 'this sweet
love of ours' in line 1 and the 'eternal pact of hallowed friendship' in line 6. But are *amor* and *amicitia* really comparable? Is
it appropriate to describe an extramarital affair in terms of the
values of the patron-client system? Between the vocabulary
Catullus uses – distinctly *Roman* vocabulary, of the public
sphere – and the private, un-Roman relationship in question, a
wide gap looms. The poem still conveys pathos, but not the
pathos of unrequited love; rather, its pathos arises from
Catullus' naive expectation that normal rules of conduct can
govern a relationship that exists *outside* the social code. This
relationship is male-female, as opposed to male-male, and it is
based on sexual passion, though Catullus may aspire to a *foedus*-
like commitment. Indeed, the Roman institution that provides
the basis for any *foedus*, the family, has no place in Catullus and
'Lesbia''s love – except to be destabilised by it.

In poem 76, Catullus more or less acknowledges the incompatibility of his 'long love' with the aristocratic social code. Yet still he is unable, or unwilling, to keep the two spheres separate. He prays that his moral conduct in one sphere – i.e. always maintaining *fides* in his relations with peers – will earn him some relief in the other, where his gestures are met only with ingratitude. The confusion of categories becomes painfully clear in the first 14 lines of the poem:

> If there is pleasure for a man in mulling over his past kindnesses
> When he considers that he's been honourable,
> And neither infringed on holy trust nor in any pact
> Abused the sanctity of the gods in order to deceive other men,
> Then many joys are waiting for you through a long life, Catullus,
> On account of this thankless love.
> For whatever things men can say or do kindly, to anyone,
> These have been said and done by you.
> But entrusted to an ungrateful heart, all have been wasted.
> Why should you torment yourself more now?
> Why don't you harden your heart and pull back from this,
> And stop being miserable against the gods' wishes?
> It's difficult to give up a long love suddenly.
> It's difficult, but somehow you've got to do it.

In lines 1-4, Catullus elaborates the first part of a hypothesis: *if* after performing good deeds a person finds pleasure in the memory of them, when he considers himself *pius* (2) and has honored *fides* and *foedus* alike (3), and has not set out to deceive other men … The *then*-clause punctures the balloon in 5-6: 'Then many joys are waiting for you through a long life, Catullus, / On account of this thankless love.' The delicate mathematics that govern Roman social relations, of services owed and rendered, is confounded in this case. Catullus has entrusted all his kindnesses to an 'ungrateful heart' and so will receive no reciprocation; his favours 'all have been wasted'.

Reason dictates, of course, that Catullus should cut his losses and free himself from a one-sided relationship. Doubtless he would not hesitate to do so in, say, a business *foedus* that had gone sour. But love is not business. As in poem 8, here the poet urges himself to be reasonable, to 'stop being miserable'. In the earlier poem, it is the memory of happier days with his beloved that prevents Catullus from severing the connection; in poem 76, that memory seems to have receded, and it is only a failure of will that inhibits him. This failure is nearly absolute, for immediately after determining that he must break off the relationship, he shifts the burden – onto the gods. 'Take away from me this plague and ruin', he implores them at line 20. He further characterises his love as 'a torpor creeping into my very limbs'; the metaphor is reminiscent of poem 51, where his tongue is paralysed (*torpere*, a cognate of the word used at 76.21) and the flame of love flickers inside his limbs. Finally, he prays to be able to shake off the 'terrible sickness' (25), and tries to strike another *foedus*: 'O Gods, give me this for my piety' (26). The Latin verb used here, *reddere*, often appears in business contexts, and can have the sense 'to pay in return'. If his beloved will not keep her end of a *foedus*, and cannot be compelled to by any social pressures, then at least, Catullus hopes, the gods will.

Lastly, it is illuminating to situate poem 76, along with 87 and 109, in the context of first-century BC Roman society. If Catullus wrote most or all of his poetry during the years 64-54 BC (between the ages of twenty and thirty, roughly), then his career coincided with Catiline's conspiracy to seize control of Rome; the rise of Pompey; the creation of the First Triumvirate, and intimations of its collapse. Perhaps in no other period of Roman history were the principles of *fides* and *amicitia* more vulnerable, was a *foedus* more likely to be broken.

Conclusion

Sirmione is a slender finger of land that extends three miles into the waters of northern Italy's Lake Garda, the country's largest lake, and a popular holiday destination. The initial impression that today's visitor may have is of a tourist trap, with so many pizzerias and gift shops crowded around the Castello Scaligero, the medieval fortress that guards Sirmione's base. But after a few minutes' walk toward the top of the peninsula all of this vanishes, giving way to quiet parkland dense with olive trees. At the very promontory of Sirmione stand the picturesquely crumbling ruins of a grand Roman villa. Standing here, the visitor is treated to a panorama of the vast, crystalline lake, with the snow-capped Alps in the distance. This may be the exact spot where Catullus wrote his famous poem 31:

> Of just-about-islands, Sirmio, and islands
> You're the dear eye-let, of everything in clear lakes
> Or in the barren ocean that either Neptune shoulders;
> How happy I am, how gladly I behold you,
> Hardly believing that I've left behind Thynia
> And the Bithynian fields, and found you safe.
> Oh what is more delightful than when, our worries dissolved,
> The mind puts aside its burden and,
> Tired from service abroad, we come to our own home
> And rest on our long-missed bed?
> This alone is reward for so many hardships.
> Greetings, o charming Sirmio; joy in your master's rejoicing;

And you, o Lydian waves of the lake,
Laugh with all the laughter of home.

This joyful homecoming is thought to have occurred after Catullus' period of service abroad with Memmius (hence the references to Thynia and Bithynia in lines 5-6), at the end of a return journey that included a visit to his brother's grave at Troy, as described in poem 101.

Compared to many of the satiric epigrams, and even some of the Lesbia poems, 31 has an extended narrative – though not following the usual order of beginning-middle-end. The 'end' of 31's story is the poet's arrival at Sirmio, developed in lines 1-4 and 11-14; the 'beginning' is his departure from Bithynia, recalled in 5-6. The 'middle' – the journey from Bithynia to Sirmio – is not described explicitly, but we know that the speaker endured many *labores* and *curae* (worries and hardships) en route. So the expression of joy in 11-14 is far from spontaneous. Unlike, say, poem 85, poem 31 indicates exactly what has triggered the poet's response. This must be one reason for its lasting appeal: it has a specific occasion and motive, so it seems to tell 'the whole story'.

Another reason is Catullus' characterisation of Sirmio, which has the same playful, flirtatious quality so notable in the sparrow poems. Catullus expresses his affection for the 'dear eye-let' almost as if Sirmio were his female beloved. He praises *her* (the peninsula is gendered feminine) as a 'jewel', and 'delightful', enjoining Sirmio to 'Enjoy your master's joy' – the imperative verb renders the peninsula an animate being, presumably a mistress to her 'master' Catullus. Then, alluding to a legend that the Etruscans (who had settled in the area around Lake Garda) originally came from eastern Lydia, Catullus commands the lake's 'Lydian waves' to laugh. Garda's 'laughter' (*cachinnus*) conveys the gentle plashing of the waves on the shore, and possibly also the sparkling of sunlight on the lake's vast expanse.

This is where the description of Sirmio ends. Which brings us to a significant, if obvious, fact: poem 31 is *not* what modern readers would call 'landscape poetry'. Catullus *doesn't* describe the panoramic view across acres of water to lofty mountains; he *doesn't* mention the wildflowers that speckle the ruins or the tiny salamanders that dart through the grass. Nor does he allude to the size or plan of his family's villa. In 31, as Eleanor Winsor Leach observes, Catullus instead

> draws the emotional experience of the poem out of the aristocratic identification of owner and house. Only from his enclosed, interior vantage point does he glance at the waters of Lake Garda, hearing their laughter as it reflects the animating presence of the master returned home.[1]

31 is certainly a successful poem in the terms Leach specifies, that is, not as 'landscape poetry' but as a meditation on the emotions associated with ownership – to use Leach's own phrase, Catullus' 'pride of possession'.

Nearly two millennia after Catullus' return home, in the spring of 1880, seventy-year-old Alfred Tennyson visited Sirmione for the first time. According to his son Hallam, who accompanied him, the old poet 'liked this [place] … the best of anything we had seen on our tour: its olives, its old ruins, its green-sward stretching down to the blue lake with the mountains beyond'.[2] It was at Sirmione that Tennyson produced one of his most graceful and affecting lyrics, 'Frater Ave atque Vale' ('Brother, hail and farewell'):

> Row us out from Desenzano, to your Sirmione row!
> So they rowed, and there we landed – 'O venusta Sirmio!'
> There to me through all the groves of olive in the summer glow,
> There beneath the Roman ruin where the purple flowers grow,

Came that 'Ave atque Vale' of the Poet's hopeless woe,
Tenderest of Roman poets nineteen hundred years ago,
'Frater Ave atque Vale' – as we wandered to and fro
Gazing at the Lydian laughter of the Garda Lake below
Sweet Catullus's all-but-island olive-silvery Sirmio!

Tennyson conjures the olive groves of Sirmione bathed in sunlight ('the summer glow'); he also mentions 'the purple flowers' growing around the ruins. He then quotes verbatim Catullus' Latin greeting *o venusta Sirmio* ('o charming Sirmio'), and, with the phrase 'Lydian laughter' in line 8, alludes specifically to poem 31's ending, *o Lydiae lacus undae, / ridete ...* ('Laugh, o Lydian waves of the lake'). Moreover, his title and Catullan phrase repeated in lines 5 and 7 create an association between the Sirmio of 31 and Catullus' famous leave-taking of his brother in poem 101, *frater ave atque vale.*

Poem 101, one of the best-loved pieces in the Catullan corpus along with 85 and 5, is an elegy – not just in verse-form, but in the modern sense too – written for the poet's brother, buried at Troy. In the opening lines, Catullus stresses the great distance that separates his brother from their home with an allusion to the hero's long journeying in Homer's *Odyssey*:

Borne across many lands and many seas
I come, brother, for these lowly funeral rites,
That I may offer the last tribute to the dead
And speak in vain to your silent ashes,
Since Fortune has snatched you away from me:
Alas, poor brother unfairly taken from me.
But now these gifts which, in the old custom of our ancestors,
Were conferred in sad duty at the graveside,
Accept them, wet with a brother's tears,
And forever, brother, hail and farewell.

'Many cities of men he saw and learned their minds,/ many pains he suffered, heartsick on the open sea',[3] read lines 4-5 of the first book of Homer's epic. There is a great poignancy in Catullus' administering of 'lowly' rites – i.e. a makeshift and belated funeral – so far away from Italy, and of course, alone. And there is bitterness in his reflection that such efforts are ultimately in vain, for his brother's ashes will remain silent.

Line 7's emphasis on familial tradition, 'in the *old custom* of our *ancestors*', conveys a sad irony, since in this instance the custom is divorced from the Roman context that gave it meaning. Indeed, the situation presented in 101 may have been charged with extra pathos for ancient readers. In the Roman world, to be buried far from one's home was to be cut off from the spirits of one's ancestors (*Di manes*), who were thought to remain on earth near their former homes; to be buried without the prescribed rites (or worse, not buried at all) was even more dreaded.

Catullus' language in 101 is formal and its pace stately, with interlocking word order and few enjambments; this high-style register enhances the mood of solemnity. Line 6 is a near-exact echo of both 68A.20 ('O brother taken from wretched me') and 68B.92 ('Alas, brother taken from wretched me'). The poet's final leave-taking, *ave atque vale*, may have been a formula used in the Roman funeral ceremony.

Returning to Tennyson's homage, ' "Frater Ave atque Vale" ' touches on two real-life events that the English laureate had experienced in common (we presume) with his Roman forebear. One of these is the journey to Sirmione by boat, which Tennyson the poet stresses with verbal repetitions: 'Row … row!/ … rowed … landed'. The other shared experience is the loss of a brother. His vocative 'Frater' ('brother') in line 7 is emphatic, occupying the first foot of the verse (and serving as the first word of the poem's title). It hints at the grief Tennyson was feeling at the time he composed the poem; he had lost his brother Charles only months before his departure for Italy. ' "Frater Ave atque Vale" ' is an elegy for Charles, and possibly also for Arthur Hallam, the best friend whose untimely death Tennyson had mourned in the poem-cycle *In Memoriam*.

Feelings of loss invariably factor into our encounters with the past. Tennyson's sense of loss at Sirmione may have been compounded when he looked on the ruins known as the *grotte di Catullo*,[4] – a visible, palpable reminder of the passage of time. Yet this ruin, this signifier of decay, is also 'where the purple flowers grow'. In the vividness of this image and the present-tense immediacy of the verb 'grow', is there a suggestion that the past lingers on into the present, that death and decay are not irrevocably final?

Catullus' readers will always feel the loss of his life-story, because his poems are so intimately bound up with the loves, friendships and feuds of one small sliver of Republican Roman society. The loss of the other neoterics' writings has not helped. Perhaps more than that of any other Roman poet, the precise nature of Catullus' achievement has been vigorously disputed. Was he heir to the Alexandrian tradition, or to the Roman comic playwrights? Was he the inventor of Latin love-elegy or a model for the epigrammatist Martial? He was all of these, and attempts to pigeonhole him (as, for example, a precursor to Ovid, or an imitator of Callimachus) too often result in down-playing his versatile genius.

Yet the incomplete historical record also has its advantages. The haziness surrounding Catullus' life has made it easier for readers to appropriate his example through the ages. Catullus, in his guises of arch moderniser, impassioned lover or fierce hater, can inspire figures as diverse as Tennyson, Edmund Spenser and

Basil Bunting, precisely *because* of his slipperiness, his resistance to easy definition. And because of the passionate immediacy of his voice, after two thousand years still addressing us as his intimates. For Algernon Swinburne, as for many others, encountering the poet for the first time felt more like recognition than discovery. In his poem 'To Catullus', Swinburne writes:

> My brother, my Valerius, dearest head
> Of all whose crowning bay-leaves crown their mother
> Rome, in the notes first heard of thine I read
>   My brother.

Notes

Introduction

1. Tom Stoppard, *The Invention of Love*, 2nd edition (Faber & Faber 1997), p. 36.

2. H.V. Macnaghten and A.B. Ramsay, *Poems of Catullus*, 2nd edition (Duckworth 1908), p. 1.

3. Amy Richlin, *The Garden of Priapus: Sexuality and Aggression in Roman Humor*, revised edition (Oxford University Press 1992), p. 144.

1. Between Myth and History

1. Roman freeborn male citizens had three personal names: a *praenomen* or first name, chosen from the eighteen in use in the Republican era (e.g. Marcus, Lucius, Publius); a *nomen* or family name; and a *cognomen*, a kind of second surname that came to be used as an individual name. Hence Catullus' full name was Gaius/Caius (= *praenomen*) Valerius (= *nomen* of the extended Valerian family) Catullus (= *cognomen*). Women did not use first names but assumed the feminine form of the *nomen*; if Catullus had a sister, she would have been called Valeria – in fact, if he had three sisters, all would have been called Valeria.

2. See T.P. Wiseman, *Catullus and His World: A Reappraisal* (Cambridge University Press 1985), ch. 6.

3. Kenneth Quinn, *The Catullan Revolution*, 2nd edition (Bristol Classical Press 1999, first published 1959), p. 3.

4. The invented pseudonym 'Lesbia' was almost certainly a gesture of homage to the poet Sappho, who came from the island of

145

Lesbos. It was also a way for Catullus to compliment his mistress on her learning and taste.

5. Quoted in Quinn, *The Catullan Revolution*, p. 28.

2. Defining Catullan Poetics

1. Because so little of the output of the other neoteric poets has survived, it is impossible to tell whether they used diminutive forms as regularly as Catullus. However, a good number of diminutives crop up in the remaining fragments. Interested readers should compare the fragments of Catullus' predecessor Laevius and those of Calvus, Cinna et al. printed in Quinn, *The Catullan Revolution*, pp. 102-4 and 110-13.

2. Catullus' use of the Latin *desiderium* in the sense of 'object of my desire' is paralleled in Cicero; still, the word's primary meaning of 'desire' comes into play at 2.5.

3. William Fitzgerald, *Catullan Provocations: Lyric Poetry and the Drama of Position* (University of California Press 1995), p. 43.

4. See ch. 3 in John Henderson, *Writing down Rome: Satire, Comedy, and Other Offences in Latin Poetry* (Clarendon Press 1999), p. 71.

3. Male Friendship in Catullus

1. David A. Campbell (ed. and trans.), *Greek Lyric*, 4 vols (Harvard University Press 1982), vol. 1.

2. David Konstan, 'Self, Sex, and Empire in Catullus: The Construction of a Decentered Identity', published online at www.stoa.org/diotima.

3. The Latin sexual vocabulary is very rich, and includes a plethora of verbs denoting different, highly specific sexual acts. For more on *pedicare* and *irrumare* see J.N. Adams, *The Latin Sexual Vocabulary* (Johns Hopkins University Press 1982), pp. 123-30.

4. Eve Kosofsky Sedgwick, *Between Men: English Literature and Male Homosocial Desire* (Columbia University Press 1985), p. 1.

4. Catullan Self-Address

1. R.O.A.M. Lyne (1980) and Fitzgerald (1995) seem to assume the unity of the poem; but Eduard Frankel and C.J. Fordyce, writing in 1957 and 1961 respectively, had doubts about the fourth stanza. Eighty years earlier Robinson Ellis sat on the fence, allowing, 'It is possible to trace a connexion between 1-12 and 13-16', though 'Such a connexion is however violent' (*A Commentary on Catullus* [Clarendon Press 1876]).

2. Ellen Greene, *The Erotics of Domination: Male Desire and the Mistress in Latin Love Poetry* (Johns Hopkins University Press 1998), p. 5.

3. Roland Barthes, *A Lover's Discourse: Fragments*, trans. Richard Howard (Penguin 1990), p. 161.

4. Paul Veyne, *Roman Erotic Elegy: Love, Poetry, and the West*, trans. David Pellauer (University of Chicago Press 1988), p. 34.

5. ibid., p. 35.

5. Crossing the Threshold

1. That 61 belongs with 62-8 is the traditional assumption, accepted by the great majority of scholars. It has been vigorously contested in recent years, however, by H.D. Jocelyn, who argues that 61 belongs with the preceding sixty poems. Jocelyn finds in poems 1-61 'signs of a conscious design' and a 'linguistic world distant from that of items 62-8'. See H.D. Jocelyn, 'The arrangement and the language of Catullus' so-called *polymetra* with special reference to the sequence 10-11-12', in J.N. Adams and R.G. Mayer (eds), *Aspects of the Language of Latin Poetry* (The British Academy/Oxford University Press 1999), pp. 335-75.

2. Catullus' lifetime and the decades preceding it bore witness to almost constant political and social upheaval (see pp. 113-14 above). The Catilinarian conspiracy of 62 BC is a good example of how shaky the status quo of the late Republic was. Catiline, a charismatic

aristocrat and demagogue, headed a major conspiracy to overthrow the government; when his plans were discovered, those of the conspirators who were found in Rome were executed without trial. (Catiline himself was killed soon after.) Cicero, who was consul at the time, believed that he had done what was necessary to save the Republic. The peremptoriness of his response, however, indicates that by this time the security of the state was a major concern.

3. For more on Roman expectations about marriage, see Sarah B. Pomeroy, *Goddesses, Whores, Wives, and Slaves* (Schocken Books 1995), pp. 149-70.

4. Compare 11.21-4, and see pp. 47 and 83.

5. So the first-century AD poet Martial warns a reluctant young man that the time of his marriage draws near: '*Flammea* are being woven for your betrothed, already the girl is getting ready, and soon as a new bride she'll shear your boys' (*Epigrams* 11.78.3-4).

6. Heather Dubrow, *A Happier Eden: The Politics of Marriage in the Stuart Epithalamium* (Cornell University Press 1990), pp. 69-70.

7. I owe this point to Charles Martindale, who also observes that the anxiety associated with marriage has hardly diminished.

8. J.W. Mackail, *Latin Literature* (John Murray 1895), p. 58.

9. Charles Martin, *Catullus* (Yale University Press 1992), p. 180.

10. Catullus' older contemporary Lucretius (*c.* 100 – *c.* 55 BC), in his epic poem inspired by Epicurean philosophy, *On the Nature of Things*, characterises Cybele in book 2 of that poem as a cultural representation of earth's life-force. '[The earth in itself] comprises the means to raise up shining crops and flourishing orchards for men's nations, and to bring forth rivers and leaves and abundant foods for the mountain-wandering species of animals. Therefore she alone is called the Great Mother of the Gods and the Mother of Beasts, and the creator of our bodies' (594-5). Lucretius posits that Cybele's retinue of eunuchs signifies 'that those who offend the divine power of the Mother and are found to be ungrateful to their parents, should be held unworthy to bring living offspring into the realms of light' (614-17). Invoking a main tenet of

Epicurean thought, however, Lucretius insists that the Great Mother (simply another name for the generative principle) is indifferent to human affairs.

11. Ariadne also roams the shore of Naxos in Ovid's *Heroides* 10. In that collection of verse-letters, most of which are addressed from mythical women to their absent lovers, a number of the heroines scan the sea, hoping to glimpse the sails of the men returning – or dreading to see their sails departing. See, for example, *Heroides* 2 (Phyllis to Demophoon) and 13 (Laodamia to Protesilaus).

12. Marilyn Skinner, '*Ego mulier*: the construction of male sexuality in Catullus', *Helios* 20.2 (1993), pp. 107-30. See p. 117.

13. Though Homer likens a young man, the dying Trojan prince Gorgythion, to a poppy at *Iliad* 8.306-8: 'And his head bowed to one side like a poppy that in a garden is heavy with its fruit and the rains of spring; so his head bowed to one side, weighed down by his helmet' (A.T. Murray [trans.], *Homer: Iliad* [revised by William F. Wyatt], 2 vols (Harvard University Press 1999). Virgil adapts the simile – combining it with the purple flower image from Sappho 105b quoted above – to describe the slain Euryalus at *Aeneid* 9.434-37.

14. Skinner, '*Ego mulier*', pp. 113 and 112.

6. The Artist in a Fallen World

1. Fitzgerald, *Catullan Provocations*, p. 140, and Martin, *Catullus*, p. 151.

2. Mackail, *Latin Literature*, p. 60.

3. Macnaghten and Ramsay, *Poems of Catullus*, p. 121.

4. The likely period of Catullus' literary activity (*c*. 60?-54 BC) coincided with the rise of the so-called 'Second Style' of Roman wall painting. This style was a significant departure from the 'First Style', in which paint and plaster are used to imitate marble. In the Second Style, architectural structures, landscapes and figures are depicted, and the illusion of depth is introduced. The most important surviving example of the Second Style is the series of paintings

known as the Odyssey landscapes (*c.* 45 BC), which were discovered in 1842 in the basement of a house in Rome. These portray episodes from Odysseus' long wanderings following the Trojan War: the man-eating Laestrygonians' attack on his fleet; his arrival at the sorceress Circe's palace; his visit to the underworld. In the episode of the Laestrygonians' attack, distant ships are painted higher, and slightly smaller, than the foremost ship in the harbour, receding into the background.

Not only do the Odyssey landscapes impart depth, they can also have a temporal span beyond one moment. The panorama of Odysseus in the underworld, notes Eleanor Winsor Leach, 'encompasses successive moments of Odysseus' experience'. So, too, poem 64's coverlet represents successive episodes in the story of Ariadne and Theseus (though they are not given in chronological order). Although we can only speculate on the relationship between 64 and wall paintings from the early 50s BC, it is not too far-fetched to guess that the poem, preoccupied as it is with the act of looking, borrowed from the contemporary visual arts. See Eleanor Winsor Leach, *The Rhetoric of Space: Literary and Artistic Representations of Landscape in Republican and Augustan Rome* (Princeton University Press 1988), *passim* (quotation above from p. 320).

5. Lawrence Lipking, *Abandoned Women and Poetic Tradition* (University of Chicago Press 1988), p. 30.

6. ibid., p. 29.

7. The Elegiacs

1. The total number of lines in the elegiacs comes to 646; the polymetrics, 848; and poems 61-64, 795.

2. Under Roman law, marriages between men and their aunts were prohibited, though unions between first cousins seem to have been sanctioned. Incest between parent and child was viewed with horror throughout antiquity. For Roman attitudes to adultery, see

Catharine Edwards, *The Politics of Immorality in Ancient Rome* (Cambridge University Press 1993), ch. 1 (pp. 34-62).

3. Richlin, *The Garden of Priapus*, p. 63.

4. For Latin obscenities as well as sexual euphemisms, see J.N. Adams, *The Latin Sexual Vocabulary*, introduction (pp. 1-8) and *passim*. For more on obscenity in Roman culture, see ch. 1 in Richlin ('Roman concepts of obscenity', pp. 1-31).

5. Richlin, *The Garden of Priapus*, p. 60.

6. Quinn, *Catullus: The Poems*, p. 402.

7. Frank O. Copley, *Latin Literature: From the Beginnings to the Close of the Second Century AD* (University of Michigan Press 1969), p. 81.

8. Macnaghten and Ramsay, *Poems of Catullus*, p. 136.

9. Some scholars identify the Allius addressed here with the Manlius (or Mallius) addressed in 68A, which aids the reading of 68A and 68B as two parts of a single poem. However the identification is by no means certain (Quinn's edition, for example, presents 68 as a single poem – but oddly retains the discrepancy in names). See John Godwin, *Catullus: Poems 61-68* (Aris & Phillips 1995) for a summary of the debate over Manlius/Mallius/Allius and its implications for the unity of poem 68. Godwin's interpretation of 68 is attractive, and a sensible compromise between the 'one poem' and 'two poem' camps.

10. Following Lee's text, the line numbers start with 1 at the beginning of 68A and continue through 68B.

11. Edwards, *The Politics of Immorality in Ancient Rome*, p. 57.

12. Anthony Everitt, *Cicero: The Life and Times of Rome' Greatest Politician* (Random House 2001), pp. 30-1.

Conclusion

1. Leach, *The Rhetoric of Space*, p. 85.

2. Hallam Tennyson, *Alfred Lord Tennyson: A Memoir* (2 vols, Macmillan 1897), vol. 2, p. 247.

3. Homer, *The Odyssey*, trans. Robert Fagles (Viking 1996).

4. For an account of historical interpretations of Sirmione's ruins, see T.P. Wiseman, *Roman Studies* (Liverpool and Wolfeboro, NH 1987).

Further Reading

Editions of Catullus

Lee, Guy (ed. and trans.), *The Poems of Catullus* (Oxford University Press 1990). This widely available, inexpensive edition includes Lee's lucid translations and some brief notes.

Quinn, Kenneth (ed.), *Catullus: The Poems*, 2nd edition (St Martin's Press 1973). Quinn's edition offers very detailed, readable notes on all the poems, and a helpful introduction. The poems appear only in Latin.

Works on Catullus

Ellis, Robinson, *A Commentary on Catullus* (Clarendon Press 1876).

Fitzgerald, William, *Catullan Provocations: Lyric Poetry and the Drama of Position* (University of California Press 1995).

Gaisser, Julia Haig, *Catullus in English* (Penguin 2001).

Godwin, John (ed.), *Catullus: Poems 61-68* (Aris & Phillips 1995).

Janan, Michaela, *'When the Lamp Is Shattered': Desire and Narrative in Catullus* (Southern Illinois University Press 1994).

Lyne, R.O.A.M., *The Latin Love Poets: From Catullus to Horace*, revised edition (Clarendon Press, 1996, first published 1980), ch. 2.

Mackail, J.W., *Latin Literature* (John Murray 1895), ch. 5.

Macnaghten, H.V. and Ramsay, A.B., *Poems of Catullus*, 2nd edition (Duckworth 1908).

Martin, Charles, *Catullus* (Yale University Press 1992).

Quinn, Kenneth, *The Catullan Revolution*, 2nd edition, introduction by Charles Martindale (Bristol Classical Press 1999, first published 1959).

Skinner, Marilyn, '*Ego mulier*: the construction of male sexuality in
Catullus', *Helios* 20.2 (1993), pp. 107-30. (Included in a special
Helios issue devoted to Catullus.)
Wiseman, T.P., *Catullus and His World: A Reappraisal* (Cambridge
University Press 1985).

Supplementary reading

Adams, J.N., *The Latin Sexual Vocabulary* (Johns Hopkins
University Press 1982).
Barthes, Roland, *A Lover's Discourse: Fragments*, trans. Richard
Howard (Penguin 1990).
Dubrow, Heather, *A Happier Eden: The Politics of Marriage in the
Stuart Epithalamium* (Cornell University Press 1990), especially
chs 1 and 2.
Edwards, Catharine, *The Politics of Immorality in Ancient Rome*
(Cambridge University Press 1993).
Everitt, Anthony, *Cicero: The Life and Times of Rome's Greatest
Politician* (Random House 2001).
Greene, Ellen, *The Erotics of Domination: Male Desire and the
Mistress in Latin Love Poetry* (Johns Hopkins University Press
1998).
Lipking, Lawrence, *Abandoned Women and Poetic Tradition*
(University of Chicago Press 1988), especially ch. 1.
Morford, Mark P.O. and Lenardon, Robert J., *Classical Mythology*,
4th edition (Longman 1991).
Pomeroy, Sarah B., *Goddesses, Whores, Wives, and Slaves: Women in
Classical Antiquity* (Schocken Books 1995, first published 1975).
Richlin, Amy, *The Garden of Priapus: Sexuality and Aggression in
Roman Humor*, revised edition (Oxford University Press 1992,
first published 1983).
Sedgwick, Eve Kosofsky, *Between Men: English Literature and Male
Homosocial Desire* (Columbia University Press 1985).
Stoppard, Tom, *The Invention of Love* (Faber & Faber 1997).

Veyne, Paul, *Roman Erotic Elegy: Love, Poetry, and the West*, trans. David Pellauer (University of Chicago Press 1988).

Wilder, Thornton, *The Ides of March* (Buccaneer Books 1976, first published 1948).

Index